D0983942

LIARS

INALIENABLE RIGHTS SERIES

...

SERIES EDITOR

Geoffrey R. Stone

David A. Strauss
GERALD RATNER DISTINGUISHED SERVICE
PROFESSOR OF LAW
UNIVERSITY OF CHICAGO LAW SCHOOL

Cass R. Sunstein
ROBERT WALMSLEY UNIVERSITY PROFESSOR
HARVARD LAW SCHOOL

Laurence H. Tribe
CARL M. LOEB UNIVERSITY
PROFESSOR OF LAW
HARVARD LAW SCHOOL

Mark V. Tushnet
WILLIAM NELSON
CROMWELL PROFESSOR
OF LAW
HARVARD LAW SCHOOL

J. Harvie Wilkinson III
JUDGE
U.S. COURT OF APPEALS FOR
THE FOURTH CIRCUIT

GEOFFREY STONE AND OXFORD UNIVERSITY PRESS GRATEFULLY ACKNOWLEDGE THE INTEREST AND SUPPORT OF THE FOLLOWING ORGANIZATIONS IN THE INALIENABLE RIGHTS SERIES: THE ALA, THE CHICAGO HUMANITIES FESTIVAL, THE AMERICAN BAR ASSOCIATION, THE NATIONAL CONSTITUTION CENTER, AND THE NATIONAL ARCHIVES.

Liars

Falsehoods and Free Speech in an Age of Deception

Cass R. Sunstein

OXFORD
UNIVERSITY PRESS

OXFORD
UNIVERSITY PRESS

Oxford University Press is a department of the University of Oxford. It furthers
the University's objective of excellence in research, scholarship, and education
by publishing worldwide. Oxford is a registered trade mark of Oxford University
Press in the UK and certain other countries.

Published in the United States of America by Oxford University Press
198 Madison Avenue, New York, NY 10016, United States of America.

© Cass R. Sunstein 2021

Library of Congress Cataloging-in-Publication Data
Names: Sunstein, Cass R., author.
Title: Liars : falsehoods and free speech in an age of deception / Cass R. Sunstein.
Description: New York, NY : Oxford University Press, [2021] |
Series: Inalienable rights | Includes index.
Identifiers: LCCN 2020030364 (print) | LCCN 2020030365 (ebook) |
ISBN 9780197545119 (hardback) | ISBN 9780197545133 (epub) |
ISBN 9780197548455
Subjects: LCSH: Truthfulness and falsehood. | Deception. |
Freedom of speech—Criminal provisions. | Social media—Corrupt practices.
Classification: LCC K934 .S86 2021 (print) | LCC K934 (ebook) |
DDC 342.08/53—dc23
LC record available at https://lccn.loc.gov/2020030364
LC ebook record available at https://lccn.loc.gov/2020030365

DOI: 10.1093/oso/9780197545119.001.0001

1 3 5 7 9 8 6 4 2

Printed by LSC Communications, United States of America

To the Truth-Tellers, Amidst the Pandemic of 2020

Some lies are selfish. Some inflate or conflate or mitigate or simply omit. Some are told for good reason. People lie because they think it doesn't matter. They lie because telling the truth would mean giving up control, or the truth is inconvenient, or they don't want to disappoint, or they desperately want it to be true. I've heard them all. I've told them all.

Michael Rowbotam, *Good Girl, Bad Girl*

Seen from the viewpoint of politics, truth has a despotic character. It is therefore hated by tyrants, who rightly fear the competition of a coercive force they cannot monopolize, and it enjoys a rather precarious status in the eyes of governments that rest on consent and abhor coercion. Facts are beyond agreement and consent, and all talk about them—all exchanges of opinion based on correct information—will contribute nothing to their establishment. Unwelcome opinion can be argued with, rejected, or compromised upon, but unwelcome facts possess an infuriating stubbornness that nothing can move except plain lies.

Hannah Arendt

When my love swears that she is made of truth,
I do believe her, though I know she lies,
That she might think me some untutored youth,
Unlearnèd in the world's false subtleties.
Thus vainly thinking that she thinks me young,
Although she knows my days are past the best,
Simply I credit her false-speaking tongue:
On both sides thus is simple truth suppressed.
But wherefore says she not she is unjust?
And wherefore say not I that I am old?
Oh, love's best habit is in seeming trust,
And age in love loves not to have years told.
Therefore I lie with her and she with me,
And in our faults by lies we flattered be.

William Shakespeare

Contents

. . .

Series Editor's Foreword

. . .

We hold these truths to be self-evident, that all men are created
equal, that they are endowed by their Creator with certain unalien-
able Rights. . . .

The Declaration of Independence

In this work, Cass Sunstein, the most-cited legal scholar in the
United States today, takes on the increasingly vexing issue of how
we should think about false speech in the modern era. The Supreme
Court has taken a rather straightforward approach to this question.
It acknowledges that false speech is generally of only "low" First
Amendment value, but nonetheless holds that it cannot constitution-
ally be restricted except in those situations in which it has tradition-
ally been limited and in which it causes substantial harm.

The Court assumes that there is no reason to encourage false
speech, but because restrictions on such speech can chill the will-
ingness of individuals to engage in true speech, we should be careful
about being too aggressive in limiting false speech. Moreover, at
least in the political arena, there is a danger in allowing government too much authority to punish false speech, because those

in positions of authority will be tempted to punish only the false speech that harms their own political interests. For these reasons, and others, even though the Court insists that false speech in itself is not something to be encouraged, it has given substantial protection to such speech under the First Amendment.

In *Liars: Falsehoods and Free Speech in an Age of Deception*, Sunstein takes on these issues with a creative and rich set of perspectives. Drawing on a broad range of insights, including those drawn not only from law, but also from philosophy, ethics, and economics, Sunstein explores in detail the pros and cons of the Court's approach and offers a challenging, innovative, and sophisticated series of observations about how we should think about false speech in the modern era. At a time when we are inundated with claims of "fake news" and when the ever-more distorting influence of falsehood on social media affects our politics and our personal understandings and interactions, this work is essential to our ability to think through these fundamental issues in a manner that respects individual decency and protects our democracy. It is, in short, brilliant, original, and deeply insightful.

Geoffrey R. Stone
February 2020

Acknowledgments

. . .

I am most grateful to Caylan Ford, Eric Posner, Lucia Reisch, Geoffrey Stone, David Strauss, and Tara Westover for valuable discussions and comments and to Lia Cattaneo, Dustin Fire, and Ethan Lowens for superb research assistance. Special thanks to Stone for two rounds of comments, which greatly improved the book. On several occasions, I have been a consultant for Facebook, including on some of the questions discussed here, and I am most grateful for those conversations; I have learned a great deal about current and coming challenges.

David McBride, my editor, offered terrific suggestions on matters large and small. Special thanks to Sarah Chalfant, my agent, for wise advice throughout. This book grows out of an academic essay, Falsehoods and the First Amendment, 33 Harv. J. Law & Technology 387 (2020), and I am grateful to the editors for valuable editorial help and for permission to draw on that material here.

This book was started in 2018, but it was completed during the coronavirus pandemic of 2020, with much of the final work done at home, during a near-lockdown in Massachusetts. During that time, the importance of telling the truth and avoiding falsehoods became, very visibly, a matter of life and death. My thanks to truth-tellers everywhere, who have saved a lot of lives.

CHAPTER ONE

Lies and Falsehoods

WHAT IS THE role of truth and falsehood in human life? In business? In health care? In politics?

Consider three problems. All of them are hypothetical, but they are based directly on real events, happening all over the world.

- Thomas Susskind, falsely claiming to be a doctor, writes on his Facebook page that COVID-19 does not create a serious health problem. Purporting to analyze the data with care, Susskind insists that unless you're at least eighty years old, you really don't have to worry about it. Susskind knows that the statement is false; for reasons of his own, he is trying to create problems in Europe and the United States. Should Facebook take the statement down, or accompany it with some kind of correction? Should public officials order Facebook to do so?
- A political candidate, named John Jones, buys an advertisement on the website of a prominent television network. The advertisement falsely states that Jones's opponent, a politician named Eric Munston, sexually assaulted a female employee ten years

ago. Jones knows that the statement is false. Should Munston be allowed to sue the network or Jones? Should he be allowed to force the network to take the advertisement down?

- Mary Winston runs a column in the local newspaper, stating that vaccinations are responsible for autism. Winston believes that the statement is true. But it isn't. Even so, the column is convincing many parents not to vaccinate their children and is thus creating serious health risks. Can the local authorities order the newspaper to remove the column? Can they fine Winston? Can they mandate some kind of disclaimer, at least online?

Is there a right to lie? About a pandemic? About health and safety? About a public official? About an actor or musician? About a neighbor? About science? If we are committed to freedom of speech, must we tolerate lies? What about falsehoods in general? How important is truth, and what should governments do to protect it?

Intimate relationships are defined by trust. ("I trust you," one person might declare to another, at a defining moment.) So are close friendships. Truth-telling is central to trust. Something similar can be said about relationships between employers and employees, or among people who work together (at, say, a restaurant, a hospital, or a school). None of these relationships is likely to be entirely free from lies, but in some cases, deception turns out to be shattering. In politics, truth-telling is not exactly universal. But in politics, some lies can also be shattering. They are beyond the pale. What can be done about them?

In a famous opinion, Supreme Court Justice Oliver Wendell Holmes Jr. wrote: "The most stringent protection of free speech would not protect a man in falsely shouting fire in a theatre and causing a panic."[1] Right now, a lot of people are falsely shouting fire in a crowded theater. They are causing panics. At the very least, what they are doing is pretty close to that. They are certainly shouting, and what they are shouting is false. In some cases, their lies lead to illnesses and deaths. In other cases, their lies cut at the heart of democratic self-government. Some of those lies come from foreign governments, such as Russia. Some of them are home-grown. They come from public officials and from politicians or those who support them.

Importantly, many false statements are not lies; people who make or spread them sincerely believe them to be true. Falsehoods are a broad category of which lies are a mere part. Some people say what they know to be false. Others are reckless; it should be obvious that they are spouting falsehoods, but they do not know that that is what they are doing. Still other people are simply mistaken; they had reason to say what they did, but they turned out to be wrong.

These differences matter. When we are deciding whether a falsehood can or should be punished or regulated, it might be crucial to know whether the speaker was a liar, or reckless, or merely mistaken. But even the most innocent mistakes can be damaging and dangerous. Consider the case of Mary Winston, who was not a liar. People make mistakes about health or safety, and their mistakes cost lives.

TWO GOALS

Notwithstanding these points, my first goal here is to deepen the foundations of what many people find to be a jarring idea: In general, falsehoods ought not to be censored or regulated, even if they are lies. Free societies protect them. Public officials should not be allowed to act as the truth police. A key reason is that we cannot trust officials to separate truth from falsehood; their own judgments are unreliable, and their own biases get in the way. If officials are licensed to punish falsehoods, they will end up punishing dissent.

[3]

As Justice Robert Jackson wrote in the greatest opinion in the long history of the US Supreme Court, "Those who begin coercive elimination of dissent soon find themselves exterminating dissenters. Compulsory unification of opinion achieves only the unanimity of the graveyard."[2]

The best response to falsehoods is usually to correct them rather than to punish or censor them. Punishment or censorship can fuel falsehoods. In some contexts, they operate like oxygen. These are time-honored ideas, but in some ways, they are now on the defensive. We need to understand them better. We need to appreciate them more. We need to do that above all to protect against government overreach—but also to allow freedom of flourish on television and in magazines and newspapers, and also online and on social media platforms such as Facebook and Twitter.

My second goal is to qualify these conclusions—and to take some of them back. As William Blake wrote, commenting on lectures by Sir Joshua Reynolds, who praised generalization: "To Generalize is to be an Idiot. To Particularize is the Alone Distinction of True Merit." Blake added, "I thank God I am not like Reynolds."[3] Aiming not to be like Reynolds, I will contend that governments should have the power to regulate certain lies and falsehoods, at least if they can be shown to be genuinely harmful by any objective measure. In brief: *False statements are not constitutionally protected if the government can show that they threaten to cause serious harm that cannot be avoided through a more speech-protective route.* I will also suggest that when actual lies are involved, the government may impose regulation on the basis of a weaker demonstration of harm than is required for unintentional falsehoods.

These are narrow exceptions. But they are important. Under the US Constitution, government can already do a great deal to control defamation. It can already regulate false advertising. It should be allowed to do more. It should be able to restrict and punish certain kinds of lies and falsehoods that pose serious threats to public health and safety. To protect the democratic process, it should be able to regulate other kinds of lies and falsehoods, even if they are not defamatory. It should be able to regulate doctored videos, certainly when they are defamatory, and even when they are not, to ensure that people who see them know that they are doctored. In defending these conclusions, one of my main purposes is to draw attention to the sheer diversity of tools. Government need not censor or punish; it might (for example) require disclosure, or some form of choice architecture that reduces the likelihood that falsehoods will spread.

I will also suggest that private institutions, including television networks, magazines, and newspapers, and social media platforms (such as Facebook, YouTube, and Twitter) have considerable room to slow or stop the spread of lies and falsehoods. To their credit, some of them are doing a great deal already, and their creativity offers a host of lessons for public officials. But they should be doing more. Real people are being badly hurt by their inaction. So are institutions, both public and private.

FAKE NEWS

If you want to ban each and every lie, or to excise lies and falsehoods from human life, you're probably not a lot of fun.

People boast; they exaggerate their achievements. Some of us flatter; we tell people things that they want to hear. People protect themselves; they lie to those who threaten them. (Do the ends justify the means? Not never; but sometimes.) Some of us joke; we tell tall tales. Journalists spread falsehoods, even when they are trying very hard to tell the truth. No one should have to live in a nation that makes it a crime not to tell the truth, or even to lie. Such a nation would crush freedom.

But some lies, and some falsehoods, are beyond the pale. Suppose that Barton Medical, a (hypothetical) company that sells medicines, markets a new product, promising, "If you take this daily, you will never get cancer!" If the product does nothing to prevent cancer, the company will almost certainly get into trouble with the authorities. This is so even in the freest of free societies. But it is not simple to come up with principles to distinguish between what is intolerable and what must be allowed. To do that, we have to explore the foundations of a system of free expression. We need to understand what such a system is for—what it is designed to do.

These issues are always important, but in the modern era, they have new urgency. One reason, of course, is the rise of modern technologies, which allow falsehoods to be spread in an instant. If you want to circulate a lie about safety or health, or about a prominent person, you can do that with ease. If you want to sell a product by lying about it, you can try, starting today. If you are a public official and you want to lie about what you are doing, you can get a large audience in essentially an instant. You might be able to do the same thing if you want to attack a public official, a former lover, a neighbor, or someone you hate or just don't like. Or consider the focus on "fake news," disseminated by both foreign and domestic agents in an effort to generate traffic, to sow social divisions, or to drive political outcomes in North America, Europe, and elsewhere in particular directions. Much news is indeed fake, and that is a major problem.

Ironically, however, charges of "fake news" are often themselves fake—making it quite destabilizing to figure out what is true. Prominent national leaders cry "fake news!" when they are subject to criticism, even when nothing fake has been said and when the factual claims are true. The real fake news is the cry of fake news. The result is that with respect to many questions, people now find themselves in a state of vertigo. As St. Augustine said: "When regard for truth has been broken down or even slightly weakened, all things will remain doubtful."[4] Or consider the contestation of science and established facts by prominent figures, including national leaders in many nations. Highly influential lies by public officials and in political campaigns are nothing new, but there are certainly a lot of them these days.

Some things are true. Dropped objects fall. The earth goes around the sun. The Holocaust happened. Barack Obama was born in the United States. Elvis Presley is dead. Cigarette smoking causes cancer. Officially approved vaccines do not cause autism.

Many falsehoods are innocuous. They are a joke, a satire, an exaggeration, a product of exuberance, a matter of "puffing," an excusable effort to impress (say, on an interview or a first date). Other falsehoods are harmful. They ruin lives. They distort people's understanding of fundamental questions. They endanger health. They lead people to take unnecessary risks. They encourage people to fail to protect themselves against serious dangers. They undermine self-government. They lead people to think, quite falsely, that good people did terrible things, or that terrible people did good things.

Suppose that in response, Congress or a state enacts a new law: The Democracy Protection Act. The law makes it a civil wrong (not a crime) to circulate or to publish false information about candidates for public office. It applies not only to newspapers and television stations but also to social media platforms, such as Facebook and Twitter. The penalty is $1, alongside an order to cease and desist. Would the Democracy Protection Act violate the First Amendment?

The answer is clearly yes.[5] But it is not clear why.[6] One of my main goals here is to offer an account of why nations protect both innocent and deliberate falsehoods. With that account, I will offer something like two cheers for current constitutional understandings in the United States. But the absence of that third cheer is important. Actually it is more like a howl of disapproval.

One of my concerns is people's ability to protect their reputations. Your reputation can be seen as part of your property and as one of your liberties. It is no light thing to take someone's property or to diminish their liberty. Among other things, I shall argue that public figures should be able to obtain redress for defamatory statements that do not meet the standards of the defining case of *New York Times Co. v. Sullivan*.[7] That decision, giving broad protection to defamation, looks increasingly anachronistic, a dinosaur in light of what is happening online and improved understandings about how information spreads.

But the damage done by false statements goes far beyond reputational injury. A foreign government might run falsehoods on social media in order to swing public opinion, to intensify social antagonisms, to promote a cause, or to weaken an adversary. A candidate for public office might lie about his achievements. A doctored video might not be libelous; it might portray someone as doing heroic deeds, when he did nothing of the kind. Deepfakes make it very difficult or even impossible to distinguish between a false depiction of events and the real thing. I shall argue that officials should have the authority to regulate (some) false statements, deepfakes, and doctored videos.

Even more clearly, television networks, newspapers, magazines, Facebook, Twitter, YouTube, and other social media platforms should be doing more than they are now doing to control the spread of falsehoods. Of course they should prize freedom of speech and the values that it carries with it. But they should also work to protect public health and safety, democratic processes, the reputations of individuals and institutions, and most broadly, the social norm in favor of respect for, and recognition of, what is true—a matter of uncontestable fact.

As Hannah Arendt warned:

The chances of factual truth surviving the onslaught of power are very slim indeed; it is always in danger of being maneuvered out of the world not only for a time but, potentially, forever. Facts and events are infinitely more fragile things than axioms, discoveries, theories—even the most wildly speculative ones—produced by the human mind; they occur in the field of the ever-changing affairs of men, in whose flux there is nothing more permanent than the admittedly relative permanence of the human mind's structure.[8]

A ROADMAP

This is a short book, but it covers a lot of ground. Chapter 2 offers a brief sketch of the moving parts, producing a framework to help orient analysis. The speaker's state of mind matters; so does the magnitude of the harm that a falsehood produces. We also need to attend to the tools that government is using. As we will see, the toolbox contains many items, and some are more intrusive than others.

Chapter 3 focuses principally on ethics. What is so bad about lying? In the process of answering that question, it provides an account of why lies can have large and devastatingly bad effects. It also has some things to say about falsehoods in general. A primary goal is to distinguish between utilitarian and Kantian accounts of why lying is wrong and to suggest that in many ways, the two accounts turn out to converge.

Chapter 4 briefly discusses the current state of American constitutional law, exploring the leading Supreme Court ruling on the subject of lies and falsehoods. It addresses the relatively recent proposition that there is, in a sense, a constitutional right to lie. One of my main purposes is to suggest that the proposition has a number of problems. In so suggesting, I aim to make space for alternative understandings. If someone running for political office says, "I am a war hero," or, "My opponent is a rapist," and if the speaker is lying, it is a fair question whether the free speech principle should provide protection.

Chapter 5, in some ways the heart of the book, turns to a large question: Why should we protect falsehoods at all? To answer that question, it investigates some time-honored arguments on behalf of freedom of speech in general. As we shall see, those arguments have a great deal of power, even in the context of falsehoods, and public officials all over the world should be alert to them. But they are awfully abstract. They do not survive an encounter with some concrete questions.

Chapter 6 shifts from theoretical questions to empirical ones. The main issue is why falsehoods are often so powerful. Why do people believe them? Why do they move so rapidly from one person to another? One reason is that human beings tend to show "truth bias": We remember statements as true, even if we have been explicitly and credibly informed that they are false. Another reason is that many falsehoods get a kind of grip on our minds, precisely because they are so vivid, surprising, and arresting. Social influences also play a crucial role in spreading falsehoods. We learn from people we trust, even if they are liars. And if we want to believe a falsehood, we might well believe it, even if we really should not.

Chapters 7 and 8 investigate the limits of free speech in the particular context of falsehoods. Chapter 7 begins with the problem of defamation. Why can't people protect their good name? As we shall see, the free speech tradition in the United States has not given an adequate answer to the question.

Chapter 8 turns more broadly to harmful speech, whether it involves false claims of achievement, false claims about health, false accusations against others, or the use of modern technology to create false images. I contend that public officials should have considerable room to protect health, safety, and democracy itself. I also contend that private institutions, such as television networks, newspapers, magazines, and social media platforms like Facebook and Twitter, should be doing more than they are now doing to control harmful falsehoods. Whether we are speaking of public or private institutions, the availability of speech-protective tools, such as labels and warnings, is essential to keep in mind.

Chapter 9 is a brief manifesto.

CHAPTER TWO

A Framework

THERE ARE COUNTLESS falsehoods out there, and along many dimensions, they are different from one another. A cry of "fire!" might be a lie, designed to cause a stampede. Or it might be an innocent mistake, coming from someone who saw some smoke from audience members who were (illegally) lighting up cigarettes. A seller of a car might lie about the vehicle's gas mileage. On a date, a man might lie about his career achievements. Someone might perjure himself, saying that he was not at the scene of the accident. Someone might make an innocent error, mistakenly identifying someone as a perpetrator of a crime.

These diverse falsehoods raise very different questions. To approach them, we need a framework. To obtain one, we need to identify four sets of issues, and we need to keep them separate. As we shall see, each of them plays a role in analysis of constitutional issues and also of the obligations of private institutions, including social media providers.

1. The first question involves the speakers' State of Mind (and hence their level of culpability). In saying something that is false, people

might be (1) lying, (2) reckless, (3) negligent, or (4) reasonable but mistaken. It might greatly matter into which category speakers fall. Under US constitutional law, it often does. The difference between lying and (2), (3), and (4) should be straightforward. The differences among (2), (3), and (4) are less straightforward, and I will explore them in Chapter 5.

2. The second question involves the Magnitude of Harm. How much damage is caused by the falsehood? There is a continuum here, but for heuristic purposes, let us say that the damage might be (1) grave, (2) moderate, (3) minor, and (4) nonexistent. A lie could start a war; that would be grave. But many lies are harmless. In deciding whether a falsehood can be regulated, surely it matters whether it is causing a grave harm or no harm at all.

3. The third question involves the Likelihood of Harm. Here too we have a continuum, including (1) certain, (2) probable, (3) improbable, and (4) highly improbable. A falsehood could create essentially certain harm, as when a seller lies about a product and thus induces a consumer to buy, or when someone prominently says, online, that people under the age of eighty cannot get COVID-19. By contrast, a falsehood could create highly improbable harm, as when a student announces in a class, "John F. Kennedy was not, in fact, president of the United States; he was actually vice-president."

4. The fourth and final question involves the Timing of Harm. Yet again there is a continuum, but for heuristic purposes, it might be (1) imminent, in the sense of occurring immediately, (2) imminent, in the sense of the occurring in the near future, (3) occurring not in the near future but reasonably soon, or (4) occurring in the distant future. A libel can easily be seen to create imminent harm. A claim, by one teenager to another, that smoking cigarettes is actually good for you might be seen to create long-term harm.

These various possibilities might be mixed and matched in numerous ways—256, to be precise. We could construct a matrix with that number of boxes, and aim to give an indication of how the constitutional issue would be resolved, or should be resolved, on the basis of what box is involved. In order not to get ahead of ourselves, and as an act of mercy, let us not to do that. Let us instead use Table 2.1.

It should be immediately clear that if we are thinking about freedom of speech, the combination of boxes will almost certainly matter. Suppose we are dealing with liars who are certain to create grave harm immediately. If so, the argument for First Amendment protection seems very weak. Suppose, by contrast, that we are dealing with speakers who made reasonable mistakes that have a low probability of creating minor harms in the distant future. If so, the argument for First Amendment protection is very strong. As we shift from the four sets of (4) to the four sets of (1), the argument for constitutional protection gains force. As we shall see, current constitutional law roughly reflects that understanding (but note: only roughly).

Table 2.1

State of Mind	Lie	Reckless	Negligent	Reasonable
Magnitude of Harm	Grave	Moderate	Minor	Nonexistent
Likelihood of Harm	Certain	Probable	Improbable	Highly Improbable
Timing of Harm	Imminent	Near Future	Reasonably Soon	Distant Future

WHAT MATTERS

To be more disciplined, of course, we need to think about each of the four scales, and about why they matter. For State of Mind, there are two major candidates. The first involves culpability. From the moral point of view, a liar seems to be a great deal worse than a complete innocent, and if people spread falsehoods recklessly, they are worse than the merely negligent. I will explore the special opprobrium directed at liars in Chapter 3. For now, let us simply notice that moral outrage weakens as we go from (1) to (2) to (3) to (4).

The second explanation points to the effects of punishment or regulation on freedom of expression. Those effects differ dramatically, depending on the state of mind of the speaker. If the state punishes a liar, the deterrent effects are far less severe than if it punishes someone who has made a reasonable mistake. If those who make reasonable mistakes are punished, a lot of people will simply shut up. But if liars are punished, liars will stop lying. How bad is that? At first glance, it is not bad at all.

It is true that the state might wrongly deem someone to be a liar. It is also true that some lies are harmless. It is true too that punishment of liars might turn out to deter truth-tellers. For these reasons, we might demand some showing of harm—at least (3)—to justify regulation of lies. But as we shift from lying to recklessness to negligence to reasonable mistakes, regulation imposes an increasingly serious threat to freedom of expression.

If we emphasize culpability, we might converge on a simple conclusion: Lies, as such, should not receive any protection at all. As we shall see, the Supreme Court has rejected that view. The Court was right on the general point. The government has imperfect tools for ferreting out lies; if government acts against lies, it might be biased, going after a particular subset of lies; human beings have a right to depart from the truth, at least in some situations. (See Chapter 5.) We might therefore insist that government must make some demonstration of harm if it seeks to regulate lies. I shall be defending that conclusion here. (As we shall see, it bears on the responsibilities of private institutions, including social media platforms.)

For Magnitude of Harm, the central idea is simple. It is no light thing to suppress or regulate speech, which means that a significant justification is almost always required to do that. A small loss is not enough. As they say, *de minimis non curat lex* (the law does not concern itself with trifles). This general proposition leaves many open questions, and I shall get to them in due course.

For Likelihood of Harm, the claim seems to be that if no one is likely to be hurt, we lack the requisite justification. Why should government regulate speech—including falsehoods—if it can show only a small chance of harm? But there is a serious problem with the claim here. Suppose that a falsehood gives rise to a small chance (say, one in ten) of a very grave harm (say, a significant loss of lives). In that event, is there a weaker justification for regulation than if a falsehood gives rise to a high probability (say, nine in ten) of a modest harm (say, a small loss of money)? What would seem to matter is the expected value of the harm, not its likelihood. I shall be defending that conclusion as well.

For Timing of Harm, the justification seems to have everything to do with the idea of "counterspeech," captured in the view that the proper remedy for falsehoods is more speech, not enforced silence.[1] If harm is not imminent, perhaps the legal system should rely on rebuttal or counterargument, not on censorship or regulation. But this idea is also vulnerable. Suppose that a harm is inevitable but not reasonably soon. How, exactly, will counterspeech help? I will be questioning the idea that imminent harm is necessary. Perhaps it ought not to be. But there is a qualification: If a harm is not imminent, we might not be sure that it is likely at all. Though officials might think that it is, they might be wrong. Their powers of prediction are limited, and their judgments might be distorted by some kind of bias. It might make sense to care about timing for pragmatic reasons: If the harm is a long way off, maybe we should assume that counterspeech is the right remedy.

TOOLS

It is essential to see that if falsehoods threaten to create harm, government can choose among an assortment of tools, with different levels of aggressiveness and intrusiveness. It might order those who spread falsehoods to stop. It might impose a jail sentence. It might impose a criminal fine. It might impose a civil fine. It might authorize people to bring damage actions in court. It might require someone— a newspaper, a television network, a social media provider—to provide some kind of disclaimer or disclosure to those who will see the falsehood. It might require labels and warnings. It might come up with a corrective strategy of its own, perhaps by telling the truth and making it readily available. Whenever free speech is at issue, courts might require government to choose the most speech-protective alternative—for example, disclosure rather than prohibition.

Private institutions, including social media providers, also have an assortment of tools. For example, Facebook, YouTube, and Twitter might remove certain lies. Alternatively, they could require disclosure. They could use the architecture of their platform in creative ways—perhaps by downgrading falsehoods so that few people see them, or perhaps by educating their users so that they can easily find out what is true. They might combine these approaches in creative ways, restricting the most aggressive for the most harmful, and the gentlest for the least harmful. In 2020, Twitter received a great deal of attention when it accompanied two tweets by President Donald

Trump, containing false claims about the high level of fraud associated with mail-in ballots, with a small label: "get the facts about mail-in ballots." (Was Twitter right to do that? I think so.)

The Appendix reprints the central practices of Facebook, Twitter, and YouTube. Importantly, governments might consider building on some of those practices, perhaps requiring their best ones. There are some promising and novel possibilities here. As the Appendix shows, some social media platforms have adopted creative methods for combating falsehoods and lies, sometimes by informing users, sometimes by educating them, sometimes by using architecture to limit the distribution and influence of misinformation. Labels and warnings might be used in lieu of removing material. We could easily imagine a law that would require general adoption and use of one of these techniques. We could also imagine a judicial holding that under the free speech principle, government is required to use the least intrusive tool. And indeed, the various tools could be mixed and matched with the four scales emphasized here—with, for example, permission to use the most aggressive tools with the 1s, and the weakest with the 3s.

I will turn to these possibilities in due course. For now, let us focus on the largest issues. Whenever we think about regulation of falsehoods, two factors matter above all: State of Mind and Magnitude of Harm. For now, however, my main goal is to point to the perceived relevance of the various moving parts and to signal that reasonable people can make different judgments about their importance. Some of those judgments turn on an answer to a single question: What's wrong with lying?

CHAPTER THREE

· · ·

Ethics

A NUMBER OF years ago, I bought a Toyota Camry after an extended negotiation at the dealership. It was a Saturday. As we started to near an agreement, the seller said, "What the heck. It's a Saturday, and so I'm just not going to sell many cars. I'll give you a really big break." That persuaded me that I should just say an enthusiastic "yes!"

An hour later, the Camry arrived, all clean and shiny and ready to drive. As I said a warm goodbye to the same seller, I smiled cheerfully and said, "Glad I could help. I guess Saturday is a slow day, and now you have a sale!" He looked utterly baffled. Apparently not remembering what he had said, he replied, with a hint of contempt: "Are you kidding? Saturday is always our best day."

After a mild of sense of shock (he lied to me!), I had to laugh. He was good at his job, and he knew something about human psychology. He did not commit fraud. But did he do something wrong?

I think so. Not horribly wrong, but wrong. By way of introduction to issues of policy and law, I will explore what's wrong with lying here. I will also attempt to defend a particular view, acknowledging that the defense cannot settle foundational questions about ethics.[1]

(Readers who are especially interested in policy and law, and not so much in ethics, are welcome to skim.)

A BIG PROBLEM

The problem of falsehoods is breathtakingly large. Untruthful statements come from countless people, with disparate motivations and diverse points of view. Some people are trying to sell cars, or something, and they are willing to twist the truth to achieve their goals. Some people really are liars, in the sense that they disseminate what they know to be untrue. They might be pathological liars. They might actually *like* to lie; lying is a way of exercising power or showing contempt. Some of them are self-interested. They might want to advance themselves. They might want you to love or like or admire them. They might be on some kind of mission. They might want to be elected. They might want to acquire power. They might want to be hired or promoted. They might want to save the world. They might think that the ends justify the means—a pervasive fact about liars.

Other people think that they are telling the truth, but they are wrong. They might have convinced themselves that what they want to be true actually is true. Their reasoning is motivated, which means that they believe self-serving falsehoods. They might be naïve or negligent, foolish or reckless, but they can do serious damage. Other people might not think that they are telling the truth. They might not really know; they don't particularly care. If a falsehood serves their agenda, so be it. That's the whole point.

For concreteness, let's put this point front and center: President Donald Trump is a liar. If we believe in freedom of speech, are his lies, and those of his allies and opponents, protected? In politics, must we tolerate intentional falsehoods, perhaps as the price we pay for freedom?

To approach such questions, it is important to acknowledge that lies are different from exaggerations, and that falsehoods are an inevitable part of life. All of us think some things that are not true, and we say what we think, even when what we think is not true. Should that be a crime? Surely not. People learn from their own mistakes, and the rest of us learn from other people's mistakes. Many of the most productive discussions—in domains ranging from physics to economics to psychology to ordinary life—involve closer approximations to the truth. To figure out what is true, we might need to hear a lot of falsehoods.

Consider, for example, what is known as "the replication crisis" in the social sciences (and especially psychology). Researchers might publish a finding—say, that people walk more slowly after hearing the world "old," or that people will eat more candy if it is in a green wrapper rather than a brown wrapper. But it might turn out that the finding cannot be replicated, meaning that the original research does not hold up in other experiments. Perhaps the researchers cooked the data. Perhaps they made some kind of error. Perhaps they were reckless or negligent; perhaps they made an innocent mistake. Perhaps they studied a small or unusual group of people. In any of these cases, the conclusion is that the research finding is a kind of junk science. It cannot be used. Did the researchers lie? Maybe. But even if they did not, what they published was, in an important sense, a falsehood.

The idea of a "replication crisis" has caught on, but we might want to reconsider the word "crisis." A pandemic is a crisis; bad or misleading research should not be counted as quite that. Still, we are speaking of deception and mistakes, and both may have a large effect on what people believe to be true. Fraud is serious misconduct, in research or elsewhere. Incompetence is not good, even if it is innocent.

Let's put the worst cases to one side. If a finding does not replicate, science is progressing. We learn from that fact. Or research might uncover some apparently general phenomenon—say, that people are unrealistically optimistic. It might turn out that this statement is not quite true, or even that it is false unless it is qualified in important ways. (After a terrorist attack, people might not be unrealistically optimistic.) If we learn that, we know more than we did before. That is how science works. And outside of science, people make progress, every day, as untruthful statements are exposed as such, or refined in multiple ways. It follows that we should not be so hard on such statements; we are going to have a lot of them, and we need them.

But lies are far worse than innocent mistakes. Should we hope for very strong social norms, reducing the number of lies to zero? Should we think of the worst lies as crimes, and hope for criminal penalties? If that seems too severe, should we hope for civil sanctions, imposing fines or allowing damage actions against liars? The best answer to all of these questions is "no." That answer is too simple, but it is mostly right. The reason is that lies, taken as such, come in countless shapes and sizes, and some of them are morally unobjectionable. Others are morally obligatory.

An initial challenge is the existence of multiple definitions of the word "lie." According to a standard definition, attempting to distill many efforts, "A lie is a statement made by one who does not believe it with the intention that someone else shall be led to believe it."[2] An alternative defines a lie as "an assertion that the speaker knows she does not believe, but nevertheless deliberately asserts, in a context that, objectively interpreted, represents that assertion as to be taken by the listener as true and believed by the speaker."[3]

These definitions are helpfully narrow. Among other things, they do not include false statements from people with various cognitive and emotional problems, who may sincerely believe what they are saying. Consider the case of confabulators, understood as people with memory disorders who fill in gaps with falsehoods, not knowing that they are false. Nor do the narrow definitions include people who believe what they say because of motivated reasoning. Such people might be spreading falsehoods, but if they do not know that what they are spreading is false, it does not seem right to describe them as "lying."

Even if lies are narrowly defined in this way, it is hard to justify the view that they are always wrong from the moral point of view. There are many compelling counterexamples. To come to terms with the ethical issues, it is necessary to engage with some foundational questions.

DAMAGE

Consider three lies. (1) John Jones falsely says that he was born on September 21, when he was really born on September 20. (2) Tom Wilson falsely reports that he likes coffee better than tea, when he actually likes tea better than coffee. (3) Mary Higgins falsely says that her first car was a Toyota Camry, when it was actually a Honda Accord.

All of these lies seem harmless. It is true that because they are lies, they appear to reflect something disturbing about the person who was responsible for them. After learning the truth, the person with whom Jones, Wilson, or Higgins was speaking might be baffled, put off, or worse. But unless we exercise a little creativity and add something to the context,[4] these lies do not inflict damage.

By contrast, the wrongness of many lies consists largely in the damage they inflict or make possible. Some lies are best seen as a kind of "taking" of people's liberty or property—in the most extreme cases, even of their life. Consider a libel, falsely reporting that someone has committed a terrible crime (say, murder, rape, or assault), or falsely accusing a candidate for public office of corruption or drug abuse, or falsely stating that a neighbor was fired from his job for incompetence, or falsely stating that someone committed terrible acts of race and sex discrimination. At common law, people have a property interest in their reputations, and a libel intrudes on that interest. We have seen that in many ways, reputation can easily be counted as an aspect of liberty. ("Cancel culture" refers to the shaming of public figures in response to their allegedly bad deeds. Many people are now being subjected to "cancellation" on the basis of lies, some of which are libelous.)

False advertising can be seen in broadly similar terms. If a car company lies about the fuel economy of its cars, it effectively takes money from its customers, at least if they rely to their detriment on the lie. The same can be said about a company that attracts investors on the basis of lies about its products, or a politician who attracts voters on the basis of lies about his plans or his past. If someone files a police report, falsely reporting that someone has engaged in assault, the harm lies in the damage done to the criminal justice system as well as to the person falsely accused. For many lies, the wrongness consists mostly in concrete harms of this kind; the lies are the instruments by which the harm is done. They count as especially horrific instruments, but that is what they are.

My principal concern in this chapter lies elsewhere.[5] What kind of violation is a lie, taken solely as such? What kind of damage does a lie inflict, because it is a lie? Suppose that a student lies to a teacher, claiming that she missed class because she was sick, when she was perfectly healthy. Or imagine that a lawyer lies to a client, saying that he has an excellent chance of winning a lawsuit when, in fact, the lawyer believes that his chances are very small. Or suppose that a teenager lies to a parent, claiming that she was working on homework with a friend at night, when in fact she was at a party. Most people will agree that lies of this kind are generally wrong, apart from the damage that they inflict, or make it possible to inflict.

Most people will also agree that some lies are acceptable or perhaps even mandatory. (Note: Most, not all.)[6] That agreement has strong implications for lies in politics or with respect to health, and also for the question of whether and when lies and falsehoods should be regulated by law. Consider the following propositions. (1) If an armed thief comes to your door and asks you where you keep your money, you are entitled to lie. (2) If a terrorist captures a spy and asks her to give up official secrets, she is under no obligation to tell the truth. (3) If you tell your children that Santa Claus is coming on the night before Christmas, you have not done anything wrong. (4) If you compliment your spouse on his appearance, even though he is not looking especially good, it would be pretty rigid to say that you have violated some ethical stricture. (5) If someone you love (say, your father) has a very serious illness, and you lie about how serious it is in order to improve his days and to preserve a sense of hope, you might not have acted immorally, though the issue is not clear-cut. (Was Bill Clinton wrong to lie about his relationship with Monica Lewinsky? I believe so, but not everyone agrees.)[7]

These cases fall in different categories. The broadest point is that "white lies" are generally regarded as acceptable, and many lies can be counted as white.[8] We lie to spare people's feelings, and that might not be objectionable; it might be an act of kindness, a mercy, even a blessing. (There are many white lies on Facebook: "Great post!") Facing serious dangers, you are entitled to lie to protect yourself and those you love (or merely like, or just want to keep safe). Lying can be a justified form of self-defense. No less than violence and coercion, lying might be a permissible way of avoiding serious threats. You might also lie if you think that doing so is necessary to help people to perform well. "You can definitely do this!" a tennis coach might say, even if he does not think that it is true; "the other guy looks tired," the coach might add, even if the other guy does not look tired at all.

In short, most people will agree that lies are generally wrong, but that in defined circumstances, they are acceptable or even mandatory. But with respect to moral questions, widespread agreement cannot be conclusive. To know whether existing ethical intuitions about lies and lying can be defended, we need to think about the appropriate foundations for ethical judgments.[9] Because of their influence, and because they are capacious, I focus on two prominent traditions here, without claiming that they are the only ones.

UTILITARIANISM

Many people are utilitarians; they want to maximize social utility.[10] It might seem that on utilitarian grounds, there is no particular reason to object to lies. Everything depends on their consequences. And indeed, Jeremy Bentham, founder of utilitarianism, embraced that conclusion: "Falsehood, taken by itself, consider it as not being accompanied by any other material circumstances, can never, upon the principle of utility, constitute any offense at all."[11] Henry Sidgwick, also a utilitarian, spoke similarly:[12]

> But if the lawfulness of benevolent deception in any case be admitted, I do not see how we can decide when and how far it is admissible, except by considerations of expediency; that is, by weighing the gain of any particular deception against the

imperilment of mutual confidence involved in all violations of the truth.

Martin Luther was not a utilitarian, but he showed strong utilitarian leanings when he asked, "What harm would it do, if a man told a good strong lie for the sake of the good and for the Christian church. . . . [A] lie out of necessity, a useful lie, a helpful lie, such lies would not be against God, he would accept them."[13]

None of this means that utilitarians are well disposed toward lies. On the contrary, they are not. Many moral strictures are easy to justify on utilitarian grounds: be considerate, respect other people's property, obey the law, or (to take an example made salient in 2020) wear a mask during a pandemic.[14] From the utilitarian standpoint, it is almost certainly good to have a strong ethical taboo on lies, which often create a great deal of harm. The taboo works to our mutual advantage; if one person feels entitled to lie, so do other people. Lies can be devastating to cooperative enterprises, and even to the very enterprise of communication. Most fundamentally, liars destroy trust. If trust is destroyed, it will be difficult for people to create and maintain relationships. As Sissela Bok puts it:

> A society, then, whose members were unable to distinguish truthful messages from deceptive ones, would collapse. . . . The search for food and shelter could depend on no expectations from others. A warning that a well was poisoned or a plea for help in an accident would come to be ignored unless independent confirmation could be found.[15]

Even seemingly small lies, within the family or the workplace, can be corrosive, because they damage subsequent interactions, producing a constant question: *Can I trust what is being said now?* Liars make it necessary to ask that question. (As we shall see, this point bears on free speech questions, though destruction of trust is usually not, by itself, a sufficient reason to punish speech.)

In the family, lying can do serious harm, certainly in the long run. Parents and children generally benefit from a strong norm against lying. If a wife cannot believe what her husband is saying, or vice versa, things are probably going to break down. In markets, sellers may well lose if they lie, because people will not be willing to buy from them. Doctors need to be trusted, and if they lie to their patients, they might not be able to be good doctors, because they forfeit trust. An employer who lies to his workers may not stay in business for very long. For these reasons, a norm against lying is straightforward to defend utilitarian terms.

Some of the most interesting and complicated liars are paternalistic; they seek to get the person to do what is, in the liars' view, in that person's interest. That may happen when employers lie to employees, when doctors lie to patients, even when politicians lie to their constituents. Paternalistic liars might be benevolent; they might be genuinely trying to help. But whenever one person lies paternalistically, there is a distinctive utilitarian objection to lying, which takes the following form. As a general rule, we might want to insist that choosers know what is in their best interest (at least if they are adults, and if they do not suffer from a problem of capacity, such as Alzheimer's disease). They have unique access to their situations, their constraints, their values, and their tastes. If someone lies to them, choosers are deprived of the (full) ability to make choices on their own, simply because they are not given a fair or adequate chance to weigh all variables. If someone wants to help people to make better choices, his obligation is not to lie to them, but to inform them, so that they can themselves engage in such weighing.

On this view, a serious problem with paternalistic liars is that they lack relevant knowledge—about the chooser's situation, tastes, and values. Lacking that knowledge, they nonetheless subvert the process by which choosers make their own decisions about what is best for them. Things are in an important sense worse if liars are focused on their own interests rather than on those of choosers. It is in this sense that a self-interested liar can be said to be stealing from people—both limiting their agency and moving their resources in the preferred direction. Paternalistic liars are not doing that, but they are assuming that they know best, and that is often false.

For these reasons, the utilitarian objection to paternalistic lying is rooted in the same concerns that underlie John Stuart Mill's Harm Principle.[16] Mill insists that the individual "is the person most interested in his own well-being," and the "ordinary man or woman has means of knowledge immeasurably surpassing those that can be possessed by any one else." When society seeks to overrule the individual's judgment, it does so on the basis of "general presumptions," and these "may be altogether wrong, and even if right, are as likely as not to be misapplied to individual cases." If the goal is to ensure that people's lives go well, Mill concludes that the best solution is for public officials (and others) to allow people to find their own path. Consider in the same vein F. A. Hayek's remarkable suggestion that "the awareness of our irremediable ignorance of most of what is known to somebody [who is a chooser] is *the chief basis of the argument for liberty*."[17]

These points apply to liars no less than to those engaged in coercion. The claim, in short, is that if you think that people are about to make a mistake, you should explain why you think so. You should tell choosers why they are wrong. You should inform them. You should not lie to them. On utilitarian grounds, the risk is that if you lie to get them to do what you think is in their interest, you will miss something of crucial importance. With respect to the conduct of their own lives, choosers usually know better than outsiders, perhaps especially liars.[18]

Nonetheless, the norm against lying, whether paternalistic or not, can be overcome on utilitarian grounds.[19] In some cases, lies are actually *obligatory* on those grounds, because they do more good than harm. For utilitarians, it is not morally obligatory to let someone with a gun know how to find the person he intends to kill. It might well be morally obligatory to lie, if the goal is to save that person's life.

In many other cases, utilitarians will not be clear that lying is prohibited, and they will have to know far more about the context in order to decide. Return to the case of a doctor who might not tell a patient the truth about the patient's condition, believing that an unduly optimistic account is in the patient's interest. In such cases, the utilitarian assessment may not be simple. We can debate what kinds of lies, from doctors, are permissible, but in some cases, deception might be justified. Or consider a teacher or a coach who distorts the truth, or lies, in order to increase a student's confidence or improve performance. We can imagine cases that a utilitarian would find difficult, and also cases in which a utilitarian would end up comfortable with a lie. The appropriate conclusion is that for utilitarians, there are strong reasons to disapprove of lying, and even to develop rules and presumptions against lying, but that case-by-case judgments are often required.

Many utilitarians are "rule utilitarians" rather than "act utilitarians." They think that we should welcome clear rules that make it unnecessary to decide, in individual cases, whether one or another outcome is justified on utilitarian grounds. Consider a specified drinking age: In principle, it might be best to go case by case, asking whether particular young people can handle alcohol, but because those inquiries would be so costly and unreliable, a rule seems far preferable. If we are sympathetic to rule utilitarianism, we might want to avoid case-by-case judgments about whether lying is justified because of the potential costs and errors of those inquiries. This is especially so when prospective liars are making those inquiries, as they may, in a sense, cook the books by overstating the benefits and understating the costs of deceiving people. As noted, motivated reasoning might well lead them in that direction. The only point is that a *universal* rule against lying would be impossible to defend on utilitarian grounds. When and whether narrower and more targeted rules are justified—say, no lying in the workplace, or no lying to one's doctor, or spouse—cannot be answered in the abstract.

KANTIANISM

Many people are not utilitarians; they believe that people should be treated with respect, and as ends rather than means. (In Kant's words: "Act so that you treat humanity, whether in your own person or in that of another, always as an end and never as a means only.")[20] Kantians think that what makes lying wrong is not that it causes more harm than good, but that it treats people disrespectfully, even with contempt. Kantians might also think that the moral prohibition on lying is absolute, or at least nearly so. St. Augustine wrote, "Nor are we to suppose that there is any lie that is not a sin."[21] Kant himself thought similarly: "Truthfulness in statements which cannot be avoided is the formal duty of an individual to everyone, however great may be the disadvantage accruing to himself or to another."[22] Kant explained: "By a lie a man throws away and, as it were, annihilates his dignity as a man."[23]

Contemporary Kantians believe that the problem with lies is that they deny agency to those who are subject to them.[24] As Christine Korsgaard puts it, "Lying is wrong because it violates the autonomy of the person to whom you lie."[25] And indeed, a feeling of disrespect captures the intensely negative reaction of people who have been subject to lies. That feeling is a large part of the perceived injury. This may be most true of cruel or self-interested lies, but it is also true of paternalistic lies. As Korsgaard notes, "Since it is my own good that is involved and I have a special right to decide what is good for myself, paternalistic lies are in a way worse than others."[26]

To appreciate the Kantian objection, suppose that your employer lies to you in order to get you to stay very late after work; that your spouse lies to you to convince you to go to a dreaded dinner party; that your teacher lies to get you to devote hours to help him with his own project. Lying is a twin sibling to manipulation, or maybe even a form of it,[27] and for Kantians as for utilitarians, it is a close cousin to coercion. Like coercion, it takes away the agency of its objects and subjects them to the will of others. And if lying is wrong because it is disrespectful and treats people as mere means, the ethical taboo might be taken to be near absolute, or at least very strong. Lies can even be seen as a form of violence. Like force, they deprive people of the ability to decide for themselves. Online and in real life, our felt reaction to lies and liars is best captured in this way.

Empirical work supports this conclusion. For example, the economist Uri Gneezy finds that in experimental settings, people not only focus on their own gains from lying, but also care about the harms that lying may cause others.[28] In a variety of experiments, he finds that the average person will not lie when doing so would benefit her by a little but harm another person by a lot. In other words, there is a moral taboo on lying that leads people not to focus solely on this question: Do I gain something by lying? Even if they do gain, they will not lie if other people lose more than that. There appears to be an implicit judgment to the effect that lying is immoral, at least if it produces losses for others. Purely self-interested lying is a moral wrong.

Even if we think that lying is disrespectful and that it violates people's autonomy, we are likely to want to make some distinctions. We might think that there is a strong presumption against lying (ever), but contrary to Kant, we might insist that the presumption can be overcome if the stakes are either very low or very high. Some lies are so small and minor that it would be excessive to insist that a moral wrong has been committed.[29] It might be disrespectful to lie to a thief with a gun, but perhaps the thief has forfeited his right to our respect.[30] As Korsgaard puts it, "We do think that the paternalistic use of force is sometimes justified," and similarly "we also think that there is such a thing as a justified paternalistic lie."[31] We might think that some lies are more disrespectful than others. If white lies are acceptable, it is because they are not all that disrespectful (they might be kind), and because they are a tolerable and even welcome part of life. Perhaps the object of a lie would agree, before the fact, to be lied to, if that is the price for (let's say) confidence or hope. For that reason, some lies might be justified on autonomy grounds.

No one doubts that a world of universal truth-telling would turn out to be quite painful. If that is relevant, an across-the-board taboo on lying would not be suitable for the human species. On utilitarian grounds, such a taboo would be morally unacceptable, and many Kantians would agree for their own reasons.

POLITICAL LIES (VERY BRIEFLY, FOR NOW)

Turn to political lying in this light. When actual or prospective leaders lie to citizens, they treat them with contempt. They deny a central premise of democracy: the sovereignty of the citizenry. Political liars do not enlist guns or spears, but they use what is, in an important sense, their moral equivalent. They act as if citizens are mere instruments for their own use.

On utilitarian grounds, the objection is more complicated, but it is not weaker. If politicians lie, they induce a kind of democratic vertigo. When citizens learn that a leader has lied to them, many of them will feel rage. After a while, they might become indifferent.

They might well tune out. In either case, leaders who lie cut the legs out from under democratic processes by making it difficult or impossible for citizens to know whom to trust. They discredit the very idea of self-government. All things become doubtful. Frances Hutcheson, the eighteenth-century philosopher, anticipated the resulting situation: "Suppose men imagined there was no obligation to veracity, and acted accordingly. . . . Men would only speak in bargaining, and in this too would soon lose all mutual confidence."[32]

TABOO AS HEURISTIC

The choice between utilitarian and Kantian approaches, in general and in the context of lying, raises exceedingly large issues, and I will rest content with a conclusion here, alongside a sketch of a position.

In my view, the utilitarian position is right. The moral taboo on lying must be defended by reference to its consequences. Those consequences are often very bad. Among the bad consequences is the feeling or perception of contempt and disrespect, which means that even if Kant did not capture the philosophical foundations of the prohibition on lying, he was keenly aware of, and highly responsive to, the psychological reaction of those who are subject to lies. That reaction is a central part of a host of terrible effects from lying, and it can initiate a host of others, including the vicious cycle of lying and distrust (and sometimes violence).

In my view, the standard objections to utilitarian accounts of lying suffer from two defects.[33] First, they fail to recognize that such accounts can and should take on board the full set of terrible effects (including the adverse effects on liars themselves, and the downstream effects of lies). Second, they proceed as if the imperfect fit between utilitarian accounts on the one hand and strong moral intuitions on the other stands as an indictment of utilitarianism, rather than a reason to question those intuitions.[34]

It is indeed reasonable to speculate that most people's moral intuitions are roughly Kantian, not utilitarian. When we are objects of lies, our assessment is often best summarized by something like a howl of pain and by thinking or saying, "That was an insult and a horrible form of disrespect," rather than, "That will lead to bad results." And on strictly utilitarian grounds, we might well celebrate the fact that we feel strong and immediate moral disapproval and even revulsion toward lies. This is a moral sentiment that increases utility. Our revulsion works against case-by-case assessments that might well turn out to be self-serving. Recall that prospective liars are not exactly trustworthy (so to speak) when they are deciding whether lying is justified on utilitarian grounds; they are likely to overvalue the benefits (to them) and to undervalue the costs (to others). They might well ignore the downstream effects of lying. And if people feel a kind of guilt or shame when they lie, even in cases in which lying really is justified, all the better. Anticipated guilt or shame probably works, in the real world, as a deterrent to lying that is not justified on utilitarian grounds.

In these circumstances, the norm against lying should be seen as a moral heuristic, one for which we ought to be profoundly grateful.[35] But as a matter of principle, our moral intuitions should not be given authority; they ought not to be taken as decisive of what morality really requires.[36] They must be scrutinized. Importantly, we are much better off when moral intuitions against lying are both strong and widespread, because lying generally leads to bad consequences. If people do some kind of cost-benefit analysis before deciding whether to lie, they may have one thought too many,[37] and they will almost certainly lie too much. But the reason that lying is bad is that it usually leads to horrible consequences, even if that conclusion does not fit at all well with our moral intuitions. To say that Bentham was right is not meant to question the moral taboo on lying, though it does force us to be clear about the assortment of consequences of lies, and on occasion to go case-by-case, recognizing that context may make all the difference.

NORMS AND LAW

An understanding of the ethical considerations is essential, but the main topic here is freedom of speech. We might agree that even when lying is wrong, it ought not to be forbidden. Indeed, we might embrace Kantian approaches as a matter of ethics, while also insisting that law should play a limited role. If spouses lie to one another or if an employee lies to an employer, people tend to rely on norms. Usually the law does not and should not intervene.[38] Nicholas Hatzis puts it well:[39]

> The fact that lying is morally wrong is not a sufficient condition for making it a legal wrong too. We wouldn't think that the government is justified in punishing every moral wrong, nor would we find the prospect of living under such a regime attractive. Something more is required before our moral failures can legitimately become the business of the state. A usual candidate is harm: where a moral wrong causes harm to another or, in some cases, to oneself, the government may have reason to act.

But return to the framework in Chapter 2. Is harm necessary? What kind of harm? What categories of lies should be regulated?

It is not exactly news to say that different nations take different approaches. In some nations, freedom of speech is not prioritized.

In other nations, freedom of speech is a defining value. But even in such nations, that form of freedom is never absolute. People are not allowed to claim, falsely, that if people buy their product, they will never get cancer. But which falsehoods are protected? I will focus to a large extent on the United States, but my hope is that the underlying principles will be relevant to nations that adopt different approaches.

For a long time, it was generally understood that the First Amendment of the US Constitution did not protect false statements.[40] Indeed, many people believed that states could prohibit at least some such statements by candidates for public office. It was not until 2012 that the Supreme Court of the United States ruled that intentional falsehoods are indeed protected by the First Amendment, at least when they do not cause serious harm. But in important ways, 2012 seems like a century ago, and the Court has yet to give an adequate explanation for its conclusion. Such an explanation might begin by emphasizing the untrustworthiness of public officials and the risk of a "chilling effect," by which an effort to punish or deter falsehoods might also in the process deter truth. But these are hardly the only reasons to protect falsehoods, intentional or otherwise. As we will soon see, there are others. We need to clarify the foundations of the claim that in a free society, falsehoods deserve constitutional protection.

In the United States, the current answers to the old questions are not exactly good. Some of them are horrendous. People's health might be jeopardized; what are we going to do about that? Nothing? Self-government itself might be seriously threatened. Is that what freedom requires? That would be an ironic conclusion. And popular answers to the new questions, emphasizing the value of freedom of speech, are inadequate. This is certainly true insofar as television networks and newspapers, and also social media providers such as Facebook and Twitter, are allowing falsehoods to proliferate. But it is also true insofar as governments are thinking that in democratic societies, falsehoods are simply part of the price we must pay for freedom. Sometimes that price is too high.

CHAPTER FOUR

Stolen Valor

I HAVE NOTED that with the help of social media, falsehoods are increasingly credible, and they pose a serious threat to democratic aspirations.[1] Russian interference in the 2016 presidential election is a prominent example.[2] As Robert Mueller's report outlines in excruciating detail, "The campaign evolved from a generalized program designed in 2014 and 2015 to undermine the U.S. electoral system, to a targeted operation that by early 2016 favored candidate Trump and disparaged candidate Clinton." Both the generalized program and the targeted operation deserve sustained attention.

In the generalized program, Russia's Internet Research Agency (IRA) conducted extensive disinformation and social media operations in the United States to sow discord and to interfere with the election. Those operations involved the spread of numerous lies. At the same time that the IRA operation began to focus on supporting candidate Trump (in early 2016), the Russian government employed a second form of interference: cyber intrusions (hacking) and releases of hacked materials damaging to the Clinton campaign. It released stolen materials through two fictitious online personas, "DCLeaks" and "Guccifer 2.0." Later it did so through the organization WikiLeaks. In fact, fictitious personae are part of the coin of the realm in efforts to blow up democracy from the inside, to intensify social divisions, and to promote Russian-preferred candidates.

The full story is chilling, and coming chapters are likely to be worse. What has happened thus far demonstrates the need for aggressive efforts, by governments and private institutions alike, to protect the integrity of political processes. There should be no constitutional objection to such efforts, even if websites and posts, by Russian or other foreign agents, are taken down, and even if their lies are simply blocked.

Private institutions also have a role to play. Facebook's Community Standards address a significant part of the problem:[3] "In line with our commitment to authenticity, we don't allow people to misrepresent themselves on Facebook, use fake accounts, artificially boost the popularity of content, or engage in behaviors designed to enable other violations under our Community Standards." Among other things, that means that it is impermissible to

> Conceal a Page's purpose by misleading users about the ownership or control of that Page;
> Engage in or claim to engage in Inauthentic Behavior, which is defined as the use of Facebook or Instagram assets (accounts, pages, groups, or events), to mislead people or Facebook:
>> about the identity, purpose, or origin of the entity that they represent
>> about the popularity of Facebook or Instagram content or assets
>> about the purpose of an audience or community
>> about the source or origin of content

That is an excellent start. But it does not directly address the problem of misinformation. Facebook's principal response is not to "remove false news from Facebook but instead" to "significantly reduce its distribution by showing it lower in the News Feed."[4] That is an important step, and it suggests the value and importance of using architecture to reduce the impact of falsehoods. People can be nudged to give more or less attention to them. But such steps are not enough, for reasons to be explored in due course.

Alarmingly, domestic political actors are replicating some of Russia's tactics.[5] To take just one example from 2019, a false rumor that Senator Elizabeth Warren displayed a doll in blackface in her kitchen began on 4chan, but rapidly spread to mainstream platforms such as Facebook and Twitter.[6] Insofar as government attempts to regulate domestic speakers, the constitutional issues can be quite challenging, and they are my main focus here.

Lies can go viral in a shockingly short time, and as we shall soon see, false statements appear to spread more quickly than true ones. I have noted that deepfakes—uses of machine learning or artificial intelligence to create videos appearing to depict people saying or doing things they never said or did—are not merely on the horizon; they are here.[7] Doctored videos are less technologically advanced, but their effects on viewers are similar. Neither deepfakes nor doctored videos make a literal statement that is false. They do not literally say, "up is down" or "two plus two equals six." But their effects are identical to those of false statements: they display something, with respect to people or events, that is not true.

On many occasions, the Supreme Court has suggested that false statements lack constitutional protection.[8] For most of American history, observers might well have concluded that the government had broad authority to punish such statements. As I have noted, it was not until 2012 that the Court made it clear that false statements, as such, fall within the ambit of the First Amendment. In *United States v. Alvarez*,[9] a badly divided Court held that the First Amendment prohibited a criminal prosecution of a person who falsely claimed that he was a recipient of the Congressional Medal of Honor.

"I GOT WOUNDED MANY TIMES BY THE SAME GUY"

The case involved Xavier Alvarez, an inveterate liar who falsely claimed, among other things, that he had been a Vietnam veteran, a police officer, married to an actress from Mexico, and a professional hockey player for the Detroit Red Wings. But he got into trouble with the law when serving as a board member of the Three Valley Water District Board, a governmental entity with headquarters in Claremont, California. He said this:

> I'm a retired marine of 25 years. I retired in the year 2001. Back in 1987, I was awarded the Congressional Medal of Honor. I got wounded many times by the same guy.

None of that was true. One part of it was also illegal. His claim to have received the Medal of Honor violated the Stolen Valor Act, which makes it a crime to tell that particular lie. Nonetheless, the Supreme Court ruled that the lie was protected by the First Amendment.

In my view, the Court said a number of reasonable and important things about freedom of speech, fitting with the framework in Chapter 2. But its ultimate ruling was wrong, even preposterous. On what assumptions does the Constitution protect an unambiguous lie about receipt of one of the nation's highest honors? To be sure, we could imagine some kind of joke or satire, or a weak moment by someone who was drunk or on a date. But Alvarez could not claim any such excuse.

Among other things, the justices who agreed with the result emphasized that punishing false speech would deter free debate and that less restrictive alternatives, including counterspeech, could promote the state's legitimate interests (such as not diluting the effect of actual receipt of the Congressional Medal of Honor). How much would counterspeech help? That is a really good question, for reasons that we will encounter in Chapter 5.

In explaining why this grotesque and intentional falsehood was protected, the plurality spoke grandly:

> Permitting the government to decree this speech to be a criminal offense, whether shouted from the rooftops or made in a barely audible whisper, would endorse government authority to compile a list of subjects about which false statements are punishable. That governmental power has no clear limiting principle. Our constitutional tradition stands against the idea that we need Oceania's Ministry of Truth. Were this law to be sustained, there could be an endless list of subjects the National Government or the States could single out.[10]

We should agree that government ought not to be given unbounded "authority to compile a list of subjects about which false statements are punishable." If Congress made it a crime to make a false statement about climate change or about evolution, or about football or baseball, or about American or German or Russian history, it would be acting in violation of the First Amendment. A Ministry of Truth would indeed run afoul of the First Amendment. One reason is that there is a difference between a mere falsehood and a lie; the speaker's state of mind matters. (The plurality elided this difference; Alvarez lied.) Another reason is that for many questions, it is right to say the government must rely on counterspeech, not on censorship or punishment. (I will attempt to defend that claim in detail in Chapter 5.)

DISCRIMINATION

Even when it is regulating falsehoods, the government needs to take the right kind of "slice" at the problem. To see why, it is important to make some distinctions.

1. Some restrictions on speech discriminate on the basis of viewpoint. Suppose a law says that it is unacceptable to say bad things about the nation's leader. Because such a law would allow people to say good things about a nation's leader, it would favor a particular viewpoint—and would therefore be automatically struck down. Viewpoint discrimination is almost always invalid, even if the speech involved is otherwise unprotected by the Constitution.[11]

2. Some restrictions on speech discriminate on the basis of content, but not viewpoint. Suppose a law says that it is unacceptable to discuss the nation's leader on Sundays. Such a law would not favor any particular point of view, because it would forbid all discussion, whatever the viewpoint. Nonetheless, it would impose regulation because of what speakers are saying. When laws discriminate on the basis of content, they are usually struck down—but not always. If the government can show that there is a very strong and sufficiently neutral justification for the restriction, it will be upheld. If, for example, a public university required classes on American history to focus only on American history, there would be no constitutional problem, even though the university's requirement discriminates on the basis of content.

3. Some restrictions on speech do not discriminate on the basis of either content or viewpoint. Suppose a law says that you cannot post signs on the subway. The law is neutral with respect to content. The government must show that it has good reasons for a content-neutral restriction; it cannot restrict speech simply

because it wishes. But so long as it can produce good reasons, there will be no constitutional problem.

Some restrictions on falsehoods would fall in categories (1) or (2). If Congress punished falsehoods that cast nuclear power in a negative light, it would be discriminating on the basis of viewpoint. A prohibition on false statements about climate change or evolution would be viewpoint neutral but content discriminatory, and so it would raise a giant red flag. With such a prohibition, is Congress trying to entrench a particular point of view? You might suspect that, and so would judges.

Apart from the question of viewpoint or content discrimination, it is always necessary to ask whether government has an adequate justification for restricting speech, even if it is false. Prohibiting falsehoods about a sport might please sports fans, but is it really important to ensure that people do not make mistakes, or even lie, about the achievements of their favorite players? If someone says that basketball great Bill Russell (my all-time favorite athlete) won ten titles rather than eleven (the right number), is there enough harm to justify censorship or punishment? In a system of free expression, that is always a good question to ask, even for falsehoods. (We will see why in more detail in Chapter 5.)

But these points do not justify invalidation of the Stolen Valor Act. Was Congress engaged in viewpoint discrimination or content discrimination? The act certainly discriminates on the basis of content. If someone said that she won a Nobel Prize or Olympic Gold Medal, she would not violate the law. The content of Alvarez's remarks certainly mattered. In a way, you might think there is viewpoint discrimination as well. If a Medal of Honor winner falsely said that she did *not* win the medal, she would not be committing a crime. But it would not be easy to argue that the relevant content discrimination, and the arguable viewpoint discrimination, are sufficient to call for invalidation.[12]

The reason is that Congress had strong, viewpoint-neutral, and content-neutral reasons for doing what it did. If someone falsely claims to have won the Congressional Medal of Honor, he is asserting a kind of achievement that could unjustly benefit him in multiple domains (including the democratic process). He is also diminishing the achievements of the actual medal winners. Allowing Congress to criminalize a false claim to have won that medal need not authorize the creation of a Ministry of Truth. As we have seen, Congress has outlawed plenty of falsehoods—for example, perjury and lying to the Federal Bureau of Investigation. Those prohibitions have not led to an Orwellian nightmare.

EXACTING SCRUTINY

Having indicated its skepticism about restrictions on false statements, the plurality said that any such restrictions must "satisfy exacting scrutiny." That is legal jargon, but the central idea is simple: Courts will be very skeptical of those restrictions, and to defend them, public officials must make a powerful demonstration that any such restrictions are justified. Officials must show that restrictions of falsehoods are supported by strong reasons, and that without regulation, government will have no other way of promoting its legitimate interests. That means that most such restrictions will be struck down. Under *Alvarez*, it is not easy to defend any ban on lies. For that reason, the decision is a great victory for liars everywhere.

Speaking only for himself and Justice Kagan, Justice Breyer called for a somewhat lower standard, one that would allow officials somewhat more room to regulate lies. In legal parlance, the standard is called "intermediate scrutiny," by which Justice Breyer meant to suggest a kind of a proportionality test, which would mean that some restrictions on falsehoods would survive. As Justice Breyer put it, the goal "is to offer proper protection in the many instances in which a statute adversely affects constitutionally protected interests but warrants neither near-automatic condemnation . . . nor near-automatic approval." That standard is a kind of balancing test.

The broader point is that in *Alvarez*, six members of the Court expressed an enthusiastic commitment to the "marketplace of ideas."[13] In one of the most important opinions in all of American law, Justice Holmes gave voice to that commitment in arguing that "the ultimate good desired is better reached by free trade in ideas—that the best test of truth is the power of the thought to get itself accepted in the competition of the market."[14] In *Alvarez*, the plurality invoked those precise words when making it plain that the Court "has never endorsed the categorical rule the Government advances: that false statements receive no First Amendment protection."[15]

We should agree that in general, free trade in ideas is an excellent idea, and we should also agree that many false statements must receive constitutional protection. But the speaker's state of mind matters, and so does harm. If I sell a car as new when it is actually used, I can be punished. If I treat your sore throat, falsely claiming to be a doctor, the authorities can fine me. If I claim to be representing the Federal Bureau of Investigation and ask you all sorts of personal questions, I am not engaging in constitutionally protected speech. Perhaps we would want to say that these are actions, not speech. Nonetheless, they are words, no less than Alvarez's claim to have received the Congressional Medal of Honor. Justice Alito put it well:[16]

As Congress recognized, the lies proscribed by the Stolen Valor Act inflict substantial harm. In many instances, the harm is tangible in nature: Individuals often falsely represent themselves as award recipients in order to obtain financial or other material rewards, such as lucrative contracts and government benefits. An investigation of false claims in a single region of the United States, for example, revealed that 12 men had defrauded the Department of Veterans Affairs out of more than $1.4 million in veteran's benefits. In other cases, the harm is less tangible, but nonetheless significant. The lies proscribed by the Stolen Valor Act tend to debase the distinctive honor of military awards. And legitimate award recipients and their families have expressed the harm they endure when an imposter takes credit for heroic actions that he never performed. One Medal of Honor recipient described the feeling as a " 'slap in the face of veterans who have paid the price and earned their medals.' "

Why, again, is a national legislature powerless from forbidding people from making a false claim to have received one of the nation's highest honors?

THE MARKETPLACE

In the relatively few years since *Alvarez*, the world has changed dramatically, not least because of the increasing role of social media and the spread of lies and falsehoods on it. As we shall see, the plurality in *Alvarez* was myopic in focusing largely on established categories of cases, such as defamation, in which false statements of fact can sometimes be regulated or sanctioned.[17] In the modern era, false statements falling short of libel are causing serious problems for individuals and society; if they cause such problems, there is a legitimate argument that they should be regulable.

In *Alvarez*, the plurality had some interesting things to say about why some falsehoods are not protected. Justice Kennedy explained that perjury "undermines the function and province of the law and threatens the integrity of judgments that are the basis of the legal system."[18] He added that "statutes that prohibit falsely representing that one is speaking on behalf of the Government, or that prohibit impersonating a Government officer, also protect the integrity of Government processes."[19] These propositions might be taken to support a much broader set of restrictions on falsehoods that threaten such processes. Should they be?

No one should doubt that for some falsehoods, the marketplace works exceedingly poorly; it can be the problem, not the solution, perhaps especially online. Far from being the best test of truth, the marketplace ensures that many people accept falsehoods or take mere fragments of lives or small events as representative of some alarming or despicable whole. Behavioral science, to be explored in Chapter 5, makes this point entirely clear: Scientific research has almost uniformly rejected the idea that "the truth of a proposition is the dominant factor in determining which propositions will be accepted."[20]

Suppose that on Twitter, an emotionally gripping falsehood is starting to spread about a high-level political official or the leader of a large company. Or consider the potential consequences of a statement in a newspaper or on Facebook about criminal behavior by a neighbor of yours, someone with no access to the media and without credibility online. The problem is serious and pervasive, and it seems to be mounting. On occasion, it results in serious harm to people's lives,[21] damages the prospects of businesses,[22] hurts investors,[23] and undermines democracy itself.

It is important to underline the last point in particular. As Justice Clarence Thomas noted, "The common law deemed libels against public figures to be, if anything, *more* serious and injurious than ordinary libels."[24] In 1808, a court stressed that "the people may be deceived, and reject the best citizens, to their great injury."[25] It is important to pause over that point. Free speech is meant, in large part, to promote self-government; a well-functioning democracy cannot exist unless people are able to say what they think, even if what they think is false. But if people spread false statements—most obviously about public officials and institutions—democracy itself will suffer. For no good reason, citizens might lose faith in particular leaders and policies, and even in their government itself. Acting strategically, candidates, parties, outsiders, or others can try to make that happen. At the same time, false statements impede our ability to think well, as citizens, about those who do or might lead, or about what to do about a crisis, whether large or small.

FIRE AND SMOKE

We can better understand the problem if we note that in ordinary life, many human beings seem to follow a simple rule: *people generally do not say things unless they are true, or at least substantially true.* We tend to be "credulous Bayesians," in the sense that we update on the basis of what we hear, but do not sufficiently discount the motivations or limited information of the source of what we hear.[26] If someone says that a doctor is a criminal, that some student or professor has engaged in some terrible misconduct, or that a candidate for public office is corrupt, many people will think that the statement would not have been made unless it had some basis in fact.

On this view, there is fire wherever there is smoke. And even if most of us are not so credulous and do not adhere to such a rule, the mere presence of a false statement can leave a cloud of suspicion, a kind of negative feeling or affective aftereffect that can ultimately affect our beliefs and behavior.[27] If we hear, "Randolph Jones never committed assault," our minds will nonetheless associate Jones with assault. In the terms of a metaphor used often in behavioral science, the parts of our mind that make fast and intuitive decisions and that are sometimes driven by emotion (often called "System 1") might credit the false statement, even if the slower, more deliberative, and more calculative parts ("System 2") do not.[28] I will return to these points in Chapter 6.

It is true and important that any effort to regulate speech will create a chilling effect. Punish people for spreading falsehoods, and you will find yourself chilling truth. In *Alvarez*, Justice Breyer noted that "the threat of criminal prosecution for making a false statement can inhibit the speaker from making true statements, thereby 'chilling' a kind of speech that lies at the First Amendment's heart."[29] Suppose, for example, that the law will punish people if they circulate a false statement about a presidential candidate. To be sure, it is good if people—voters as well as the candidate personally—are not injured as a result of that false statement. But that very law will discourage others from disclosing, on the basis of credible evidence, the fact that a candidate has done something wrong or even terrible.

But there is a countervailing consideration. Sometimes a chilling effect can be an excellent safeguard. Without such an effect, the marketplace of ideas will allow many people to spread damaging falsehoods about both individuals and institutions. If false statements create serious problems, it is important to ensure that the fear of a chilling effect does not itself have a chilling effect on public discussion or on social practices. Some falsehoods can hurt or even ruin individual lives. For all these reasons, it is sensible to hope that social norms and even law will chill them. We need, in short, to find ways to discourage the spread of statements that are at once false and damaging.

CHAPTER FIVE

Truth

WHY ARE (SOME) falsehoods protected by the First Amendment? Consider a few examples:

> "The moon landing was faked." "Pigs really can fly." "The United States military carried out the 9/11 attacks." "The stock market is at an all-time low." "Ruth Bader Ginsburg is Chief Justice of the United States Supreme Court." "Dropped objects don't fall." "Bob Dylan did not write any songs." "The Holocaust never happened." "The real unemployment rate in the United States is at least 70 percent." "Senator Elizabeth Warren is a Russian agent—bought and paid." "Plastic is a kind of gold." "Dogs are descended from coyotes, not wolves." "The Earth is flat." "The Easter Bunny is real." "The US Constitution was ratified in 1727." "The plays of William Shakespeare were written by Albert Camus."

Many people believe some of these propositions. Let us stipulate that all of them are demonstrably false. Why should they be protected? The most famous discussion, and in some ways still the best, comes from John Stuart Mill.[1] We have already seen that some falsehoods, specifically those that are not typically subject to regulation, have unmistakable value. White lies spare people's feelings, and people might lie to ward off threats. As Justice Breyer put it in *United States v. Alvarez*: "False factual statements can serve useful human objectives. . . . [T]hey may prevent embarrassment, protect privacy, shield a person from prejudice, provide the sick with comfort, or preserve a child's innocence; . . . they may stop a panic or otherwise preserve calm in the face of danger; and even . . . can promote a form of thought that ultimately helps realize the truth."[2] Mill emphasized the latter point, that is, the role of falsehoods in helping truth. But his discussion, brief though it was, was wide ranging.

I shall draw on that discussion here. But as we shall see, Mill's arguments run into serious problems. They are too abstract and high flown to resolve hard questions, including those posed by defamation, deepfakes, doctored videos, and genuinely damaging falsehoods in general. As applied to such questions, they sound a lot better than they actually are.

Before exploring that objection, it is important to emphasize that in well-functioning societies, restrictions on lying and safeguards against spreading falsehoods come mostly from social norms, not from law. If you fail to tell the truth, you are likely to face social punishments of various kinds.[3] People are aware of that risk in advance, and so they generally internalize the norm in favor of honesty, such that they feel shame or guilt if they violate it. In addition, people know that if they lie, their rivals or opponents might lie as well, and a norm in favor of truthfulness avoids a kind of mutual destruction.[4] When things are going well, social norms do the work of law. When norms punish lying or the spread of falsehoods, there is much less pressure on the legal system to intervene.

In this light, we should see the use of the common law and regulatory interventions as a response to the imperfect power of norms in certain contexts. We can even think of the need for law as a demonstration of the failure of social norms. Consider the case of defamation. If you lie and damage the reputation of your neighbor, or a fellow member of the human race, you might well lose your own standing. Because you know that, you might refrain from lying. Things go sour when norms break down, and when they do, there will be increasing pleas for a more aggressive legal response.

Imagine that in certain sectors, norms only weakly favor truth-telling, and that reputational, economic, political, or other incentives favor lying. Or suppose it is easy for people to speak anonymously or otherwise to avoid disclosure of their identities, and having done so, they lie. If so, many people will want the legal system to respond. They might be right. In some cases, they surely are.

THE VALUE OF FREE SPEECH

But how shall we decide whether certain speech is protected by the First Amendment? Or by the best understanding of the very idea of freedom of speech? In the abstract, it might not be at all clear how to handle bribery, obscenity, commercial advertising, libel, criminal solicitation, criminal conspiracy, hate speech, falsehoods in general, or lies in particular. If we are asking the constitutional question, some people would insist on "originalism"; they would ask about the original public understanding of the constitutional text. Some prominent judges think that constitutional problems, including the scope of the First Amendment, are best solved by reference to that question. I am not going to try to make historical claims here, but there is a good argument that for originalists, many falsehoods would not deserve constitutional protection.[5] But most judges are not originalists. If we reject originalism, we might be interested in obtaining an understanding of what kinds of values the idea of freedom of speech is best taken to promote.

There is a great deal of disagreement on how to answer that question. Some people insist that the answer lies in democratic ideals.[6] In their view, there is an inextricable relationship between free speech and self-government. For people who embrace this view, many falsehoods, and many lies, are unprotected by the free speech principle, because they have nothing to do with self-government. ("Elvis Presley is alive and living in Hawaii." "I won the local golf tournament." "My neighbor, Warren Crisp, killed his cat last night.") Other people think that the free speech principle is about individual autonomy.[7] On that view, freedom of speech has intrinsic rather than instrumental value. It is part of what it means to be autonomous; it is not protected because of its consequences. If this is what we believe, we might well protect falsehoods, at least presumptively; it is a fair question whether we would protect lies.

On another view, freedom of speech is protected because (as Holmes thought) the marketplace of ideas is the best way of discovering truth. If we embrace that idea, we might not be sure how to handle falsehoods and lies; there are arguments both ways. But on plausible assumptions, we might also adopt a presumption in favor of protecting falsehoods, and perhaps lies as well. After all, falsehoods can help us discover what is true. (Maybe.) On another view, we protect freedom of speech because speech is the principal mechanism or vehicle by which we communicate or cooperate with one another.[8] Those who adopt this understanding might want to protect falsehoods, but not lies. As Seana Shiffrin puts it, "Deliberately insincere speech should not garner the same sort of respect because it does not participate, even at the fringe, in the same values as sincere or transparent speech."[9]

I do not aim here to choose among these competing understandings. For the most part, I will focus more eclectically on why a sensible Constitution might refuse to allow regulation or censorship of falsehoods. Some of those arguments point to the relationship between free speech and self-rule ("We the People"); others invoke the marketplace of ideas; others speak of autonomy. In general, however, the arguments are utilitarian in spirit. They consist of objections to what the world would turn out to be like if we allowed regulation of falsehoods.

OFFICIALS CANNOT BE TRUSTED

If public officials are allowed to punish or censor what they characterize as false, they might end up punishing or censoring truth. The reason is that their own judgments may not be reliable. They might be foolish or ignorant. However confident, they might be wrong. Worst of all, their judgments are likely to be self-serving. If a president, chancellor, or prime minister tries to censor speech as "fake news," the real reason might not be that it is fake. The real reason might be that it casts them in a bad light. The truth police are often minions of an authoritarian, trying to keep a hold on power. A more particular problem is "discretionary charging": Officials go after those lies and falsehoods that put them in a bad light, and ignore or celebrate those that put them in a good light.

In defending the right to say what is false, Mill made this point gently, arguing that those who seek to suppress speech "of course deny its truth; but they are not infallible. . . . All silencing of discussion is an assumption of infallibility."[10] Actually that is too gentle. To support Mill's point, we should make a distinction between innocent error on the one hand and authoritarianism, or something like it, on the other. Officials might want to suppress scientific findings, sincerely but wrongly believing that those findings are false and also harmful. When Galileo was persecuted for claiming that the earth goes around the sun, rather than vice versa, his persecutors were perfectly sincere; they were clear in their own minds that Galileo was wrong.

By contrast, authoritarian leaders, censoring accurate accounts of what they have done, have no illusions about what actually happened. They want to suppress the truth. Some of the most interesting cases are mixed. A leader may believe that he is being victimized by fake news, but his belief may be motivated; he wants to believe that the story is untrue, and he succeeds in acquiring that belief. He tries to engage in censorship for that reason. And again he is concerned about a specific subclass of lies and falsehoods: Those that put him in an unfavorable light or jeopardize his goals or threaten his power.

For a case in point, or a series of such cases, consider the official reaction to freedom of speech during the COVID-19 pandemic of 2020. More than twenty nations responded to the pandemic by limiting speech, often on the reasonable theory that the limitations were necessary to prevent the dissemination of falsehoods that would cost lives.[11] Nominally the goal was to counteract an "infodemic" that aggravated the public health crisis, and in many cases, that was indeed the goal. In Taiwan, for example, the government took strong steps to stop misinformation about the disease, which might well be justified (see Chapter 7). But in some countries, the law went much further.

In Thailand, for example, Prime Minister Prayut Chan-o-cha issued an emergency decree, prohibiting publication of information that "may instigate fear amongst the people or is intended to distort information which misleads understanding of the emergency situation to the extent of affecting the security of state or public order or good morale of the people." The law was extended to criticisms of the government's own performance. In the same vein, the government of Hungary enacted a law authorizing three-year prison sentences for anyone convicted of spreading falsehoods about the virus that are "alarming or agitating [to] a large group of people"— and allowing five-year sentences for anyone convicted of spreading a falsehood or "distorted truth" with harmful consequences for public health. The government of Bolivia issued its own emergency decree, allowing criminal penalties against "individuals who incite noncompliance with this decree or misinform or cause uncertainty to the population." Causing "uncertainty" is a vague crime, and it is likely that laws of this sort would be used to attack dissenters. In such cases, official fallibility includes simple error on the part of officials; but it also points to self-interested motives.

On Mill's view, official fallibility is a sufficient reason to ensure that we protect what officials deem to be falsehoods—and that we allow public discussion and counterspeech to provide a corrective, if a corrective is what is needed. That argument has immense power. Human history suggests that when officials seek to punish or block falsehoods, their real concern is dissent, not falsehoods. In connection with the COVID-19 pandemic, an especially vivid example comes from China. Dr. Wenliang Li was a whistleblower who drew attention to the danger. In 2020, he was disciplined for "spreading misinformation." (He eventually died of the virus.) In general, the right reaction to Mill's emphasis on the "assumption of infallibility" is an enthusiastic nod of the head and a standing ovation.

But in important cases, Mill's claim is unconvincing, and obviously so. Imagine that someone perjures himself in a criminal case. Is perjury protected by the Constitution? We can emphasize all we like that the legal system is fallible and that it does not have perfect tools for deciding whether someone has, in fact, committed perjury. But it would be pretty foolish to conclude that the legal system should allow perjury.

Or imagine that officials are trying to ban a false advertisement, claiming that if you take the red pill, you will never get coronavirus, and if you take the blue one too, you will forever be free from heart disease. Or imagine that someone falsely accuses a neighbor of rape. Does Mill's argument suggest that the accusation may not be punished? Or imagine that a seller of real estate falsely tells a potential buyer, "We just got five offers for this house—all above the purchase price!" Or suppose someone claims that he is an agent of the Federal Bureau of Investigation (FBI), when he is nothing of the sort; he lies in order to get access to confidential information. Is that lie protected by the very idea of freedom of speech?

These examples suggest that official fallibility should not be taken as a trump card, allowing lies and falsehoods regardless of the context, or of their effects. A key question is whether we can create reliable institutions and draw appropriate lines. More specifically, it is whether we might be able to specify categories of harmful falsehoods, and insist that they can be restricted, while also creating safeguards to reduce the risk of official errors to a tolerable degree.

One such safeguard, and perhaps the most important, is an independent tribunal. A court, free from political pressures and not subject to the control of any president or prime minister, should be the institution to resolve the question of truth or falsity. If an independent court is in charge of the proceedings, the risk of bias should be significantly reduced. To be sure, courts themselves are not infallible. Their fact-finding tools are hardly perfect, and they might well have biases of their own. In the worse cases, they are unduly sympathetic to political officials, which means that even if they will not do their bidding, they will usually rule as such officials like. If that is so, they are not truly independent. The only point is that an independent tribunal can serve as an important check on the potentially self-serving judgments of others, including executive officials.

Another safeguard is the burden of proof. With what clarity must it be shown that a statement is in fact false? Even if officials are fallible, a high burden of proof will diminish the risk of unjustified restrictions on speech. If we are very concerned about the risk of error, we might insist that falsehoods may be punished or censored *only when an independent tribunal has concluded that there is no reasonable doubt about the matter*—as, for example, when someone has been defamed with an unmistakably false claim or accusation. If a person who claims to have been defamed must show "clear and convincing evidence" that the allegedly defamatory statement was false, or must demonstrate that the statement was false "beyond a reasonable doubt," the danger of official error or bias is diminished. The same is true if, for example, someone makes a claim about public health, and about what works to save lives, that seems to be false (and potentially dangerous).

In short: As the burden of proof grows increasingly difficult to meet, Mill's argument about the dangers of official error becomes increasingly weak. If someone says that a university president is a cocaine addict, and if it is proved beyond a reasonable doubt that she really isn't, should we really let the statement go, on the ground that officials might err? It would not be easy to justify an answer of "yes." At the same time, a high burden of proof should also reduce the risk that true statements will be chilled. Speakers have much less to worry about if they will not be held accountable unless it is 100 percent clear that they have spread a falsehood.

In direct response to Mill's claim, we should reiterate that many democratic nations, including the United States, have long forbidden various kinds of falsehoods, including perjury,[12] false advertising,[13] and fraud.[14] People are not allowed to say that they are agents of the FBI unless they actually are.[15] In these cases, Mill's argument has been rightly and thoroughly rejected. It is true that in such cases, there is usually demonstrable harm, and it makes sense to say that false statements are protected unless there is such harm, or at least a significant risk of that (a question to which I will return). But the question here is whether Mill's argument about official fallibility is, by itself, a convincing reason to protect falsehoods. It is not.

The most plausible argument in defense of Mill's position, or using it more than most legal systems now do, would take the following form. Perhaps the risk of official error (including judicial error) is high—not always, but much of the time. Perhaps case-by-case inquiries into the question of truth or falsity would be burdensome and time-consuming. Perhaps we do best to avoid those inquiries and conclude that officials cannot punish or censor falsehoods unless they can make a powerful showing of grave harm.

That argument is not implausible in the abstract, but it too is unconvincing, at least in well-functioning legal systems. We should be able to agree that there is no point in regulating speech unless it is harmful. But if falsehoods are indeed harmful, should they be protected merely because officials are fallible? If people lie to the Federal Bureau of Investigation about their employment history, or falsely claim to be a government agent when trying to frighten a neighbor, or write in a job application for state employment that they competed in the Olympics, is it so clear that the First Amendment should be taken to prohibit punishment, even if the harm done by those lies is not grave?

CHILLING TRUTH

A different reason to protect falsehoods has nothing to do with official fallibility. It is that allowing government to punish or censor what is false might deter people from saying what is true.

Suppose you are told that if you say something false, you will have to pay a significant fine. You might not speak at all. You might decide to steer well clear of the line, meaning that you will shut up about a range of things that are actually true. Or suppose a legislature enacts a new law, a Truth in Politics Act, making it a crime for a newspaper or magazine to publish any falsehood about a candidate for public office. Journalists would undoubtedly self-silence even if what they have to say is both truthful and important.

As four justices put it in *Alvarez*:

> Were the Court to hold that the interest in truthful discourse alone is sufficient to sustain a ban on speech, . . . it would give government a broad censorial power unprecedented in this Court's cases or in our constitutional tradition. The mere potential for the exercise of that power casts a chill, a chill the First Amendment cannot permit if free speech, thought, and discourse are to remain a foundation of our freedom.[16]

So much, in this light, for any Truth in Politics or Democracy Protection Act.

For all of us, the mere possibility of a criminal or civil proceeding might induce self-silencing. To be sure, this problem could be reduced if the legal system had a perfect technology for detecting falsehoods. In a science fiction world (and perhaps it is coming), the law would be able to tell, for sure, whether a statement is true or false, and it would never punish truth. If so, people could be perfectly confident that so long as they told the truth, they could not be punished.

That would be an advance, but it would not be close to enough to protect freedom of speech. The reason is that with many of our statements, we are not certain. We have *degrees of certainty*. We believe that the earth goes around the sun, but we are not entirely sure. We think that our favorite politician is not guilty of the latest charge against her, but we are not certain. We think that childhood vaccinations do not cause autism, and perhaps we are very confident of that, but we might feel a shadow of a doubt. For much of what we say, even in public, we might be 51 percent confident, 60 percent confident, 80 percent confident, or 95 percent confident.

Even journalists have different degrees of confidence and different thresholds for having enough confidence to speak or write. If falsehoods were punishable, people might not speak out unless they are essentially certain—which would be a significant loss to speakers and to society as a whole. In the face of potential punishment, people might stay quiet, even when what they think is right. What kind of democracy, and what kind of society, insists that people shut up unless they *know* that they are right?

Justice Stephen Breyer may well have something like this point in mind in insisting that "laws restricting false statements about philosophy, religion, history, the social sciences, the arts, and the like raise [serious] concerns, and in many contexts have called for strict scrutiny."[17] Justice Alito rightly combined that point with Mill's concern about institutional fallibility:

> There are broad areas in which any attempt by the state to penalize purportedly false speech would present a grave and unacceptable danger of suppressing truthful speech. Laws restricting false statements about philosophy, religion, history, the social sciences, the arts, and other matters of public concern would present such a threat. The point is not that there is no such thing as truth or falsity in these areas or that the truth is always impossible to ascertain, but rather that it is perilous to permit the state to be the arbiter of truth.[18]

This is an important claim. We can fortify it by emphasizing that (true) information confers benefits on society as a whole, not merely on speakers. If someone discloses something of importance, many people will benefit. We protect speech in large part because of the countless citizens who gain if they can hear what other people have to say. Of course we can question whether falsehoods help anyone (a point to which I will return)—but if suppressing them suppresses truth too, we might tolerate a lot of falsehoods, not for the benefit of the speaker, but for the benefit of all of us. The point is nicely captured by Joseph Raz:

> If I were to choose between living in a society which enjoys freedom of expression, but not having the right myself, or enjoying the right in a society which does not have it, I would have no hesitation in judging that my own personal interest is better served by the first option.[19]

When free speech principles are designed to protect against a chilling effect, speakers gain of course. They don't have to be frightened of the authorities. That is important. But an even larger goal is to help unknown and unknowable others.

All that might be right, but before considering a chilling effect to be decisive, let us pause for a moment. Is a chilling effect really a sufficient reason to protect lies and other falsehoods? All of them? Why should a chilling effect be a trump card? No one thinks that the ban on perjury should be lifted because it also chills truthful testimony (though it undoubtedly does at least a little of that). It is a bit wild to think that a ban on false commercial advertisements should be lifted because it also chills truthful commercial advertising (though it undoubtedly does at least a little of that). If you tell people that they can't impersonate federal officers, you might chill some truth, but that's really not a big problem. A revealing technicality: The Supreme Court has allowed a construction contractor to bring a defamation action against a credit reporting agency for falsely reporting that the contractor had filed for bankruptcy.[20] The Court's decision will probably deter true statements, not just false ones. But that's not a good enough reason to allow the false ones.

Or suppose that what is chilled contains a great deal of falsity and a small amount of truth. What is chilled is 98 percent false and 2 percent true. If so, it is hardly clear that a ban on falsity is unjustified. To know how to think about a chilling effect, we would need to know its size and then the harm produced by chilling truth, along with the benefit produced by chilling falsehood. The fact that banning falsity chills truth is a relevant consideration, and it is often decisive. We should start with it. But it is not enough to justify the proposition that all false statements should be protected as free speech.

What is necessary, in short, is optimal chill—the right level of deterrence, considering what happens to both falsehoods and truths. If an approach chills a very large number of very damaging falsehoods and a small number of not-very-important truths, we should probably adopt it. Recognition of a chilling effect on truth is important, but it does not tell us how to get close to the point of optimal chill.

LIVING TRUTHS

Suppose that government could be trusted; suppose too that any chilling effect on truth would be modest or inconsequential. If so, ought we allow censorship of false statements of fact? That question raises this one: Do unquestionably false statements have social value? The Supreme Court has often said that they do not, but maybe that's wrong. Put to one side the case of white lies, or lies that are necessary to prevent harm. Perhaps false statements—about, say, history or science—are helpful to those of us who know what is true. Perhaps they are even essential to us, even if we are clear about the facts. A strong possibility, signaled by Mill, is that false statements can improve our understanding:

[65]

However unwillingly a person who has a strong opinion may admit the possibility that his opinion may be false, he ought to be moved by the consideration that however true it may be, if it is not fully, frequently, and fearlessly discussed, it will be held as a dead dogma, not a living truth. . . . If the cultivation of the understanding consists in one thing more than in another, it is surely in learning the grounds of one's own opinions. . . . He who knows only his own side of the case, knows little of that. His reasons may be good, and no one may have been able to refute them. But if he is equally unable to refute the reasons on the opposite side, if he does not so much as know what they are, he has no ground for preferring either opinion.[21]

Surely it is better to hold a living truth than a dead dogma, and if people say something false (and horrible), our convictions about what is true might catch fire, in a good and productive way. Mill added a separate point, which is that false statements can bring about "the clearer perception and livelier impression of truth, produced by its collision of error."[22] Mill's point holds for a large number of false statements. If people are told that the moon landing was faked or that the Holocaust never happened, they can learn more about the truth of these matters—but only if the statements are not censored. Consider a classroom. If students make mistakes, the discussion might well be improved. Falsehoods put a spotlight on truth. They give it life.

In general, Mill's point is right. It is sufficient to suggest that falsity, by itself, should not be taken to be a *decisive* reason to allow punishment or censorship. But back to one of our broader themes: For many problems, Mill's argument is impossibly abstract and high-minded. For one thing, it may not apply to lies at all.[23] Mill's own concern was limited to cases in which people were saying what they actually thought. Suppose a politician proclaims that he won the Congressional Medal of Honor when he did not. Should we say that the politician's lie helped people to discover a "living truth"? If someone impersonates a police officer, is it a good idea to force people to find out that he is doing that?[24] Should the impersonation be allowed, on the ground that it promotes learning? Or suppose that someone falsely tells a federal investigator that an applicant for federal employment is a cocaine addict. Should the statement be allowed, because the investigator can learn that the statement is false? As Shiffrin puts it, "It is difficult to extrapolate from the right of the sincere to attempt to persuade others of what they believe, to a right of the insincere to engage in deliberate misrepresentation."[25]

It is true that liars can prompt people to think more and better. If someone lies about whether a medicine actually works, about American history, or about climate change, he can initiate a process of rethinking and learning. That process fits with Mill's argument. We can take this point to support the proposition that lies should not be punished unless they create harm. But what if they do?

Taken on its own terms, Mill's argument is undermined by the fact that human beings have limited time and attention.[26] The sheer effort required to discover whether a statement is true or false may mean that people will simply believe it, certainly if it fits with their antecedent convictions.[27] The existence of online echo chambers, in which many people sort themselves into groups of the like-minded, compounds the problem. (We'll get to that.)

Mill was right to say that people can learn from false statements and that living truths are far better than dead dogmas. He was correct to emphasize that falsehoods keep people on their toes, and so keep truths alive. But here again, his argument does not provide a convincing basis for protection of all falsehoods, intentional or otherwise—and the argument is palpably inadequate when falsehoods threaten to produce clear and imminent harm.

LEARNING WHAT OTHERS THINK

There is a related point, not emphasized by Mill. When people hear falsehoods, they can learn more about what other people think, and why. If people find out that many of their fellow citizens believe that coronavirus is a hoax, that vaccines cause autism, that President Barack Obama was not born in the United States, or that the United States was responsible for the attacks of 9/11, they will learn something that it is important to know. "Pluralistic ignorance," understood as ignorance about what other people actually think, can be a serious problem.[28]

If falsehoods can be spoken and written, people will be better able to obtain a sense of the distribution of views within their society—of what others actually believe. That can be a large benefit. For one thing, it can give people a sense that their own views might not be quite right; it can crack a wall of certainty. Apart from that point, it can provide people with valuable information. If many of your fellow citizens believe that the earth is flat or that climate change is a hoax invented by the Chinese government, you benefit from obtaining that knowledge.

Again, this is not a decisive argument in favor of allowing any and all falsehoods. It works best for false beliefs that are sincerely held; it is much harder to understand the argument as a reason to protect lies. The argument does not justify protection of perjury and false advertising. And even for sincerely held false beliefs, it is inadequate. The benefit of learning what others think might be outweighed by the cost of allowing falsehoods to spread. The only point is that it is a benefit.

COUNTERSPEECH > BANS

The final point is intensely pragmatic. Banning or punishing falsehoods might simply drive beliefs underground. They might not be exposed to the light. They can be fueled by the very fact that they are forbidden. If the goal is to reduce their power, allowing falsehoods to have some oxygen, and forcing people to meet them with counterarguments, might be best.

A law might forbid denial of the Holocaust, as German law does, and in view of German history, such a law might be a reasonable idea. Holocaust denial might fuel anti-Semitism, and perhaps a prohibition reduces real risks. But in the abstract, we cannot rule out the possibility that from the standpoint of the very people who support that prohibition, freedom of speech would be better. One reason is that suppression of speech might intensify people's commitment to the very falsehoods that it contains. Another reason is that suppression might create a kind of forbidden fruit, broadening the appeal of those falsehoods. Yet another reason is that suppression might be taken as an attack on individual autonomy. Isn't it better to convince people rather than to shut them up?

The now-familiar response is that these points are far too abstract to resolve concrete cases. With respect to Holocaust denial, is oxygen a good idea? In Germany? In every nation? That is hardly clear. Nor is it clear that it applies to lies about what people have said or done. Consider *Alvarez* itself: If someone falsely claims to have won the Congressional Medal of Honor, is it really such a bad idea to drive that claim underground? When people do not believe what they are saying, it is hard to justify the proposition that their lies need to be protected lest they be driven underground.

HARM IN THE BALANCE

Return to the framework in Chapter 2. When falsehoods are banned, it is not only because they are falsehoods, but also because they threaten to produce real harm. A false cry of "fire!" in a crowded

theater is not merely false. It also threatens, with a high probability, to cause serious harm—and under plausible assumptions,
little or nothing can be done, in time, to prevent that harm. Some
falsehoods create a clear and present danger.[29] That test, orig-
inally understood to allow a great deal of regulation, is generally
understood to have been replaced by the far more stringent test in
Brandenburg v. Ohio,[30] where the Court struck down a law making it
a crime to "advocat[e] . . . the duty, necessity, or propriety of crime,
sabotage, violence, or unlawful methods of terrorism as a means of
accomplishing industrial or political reform." The *Brandenburg* test
is highly protective of speech. Under that test, regulation is permissible only if (1) the speech is intended to produce imminent lawless
action *and* (2) it is likely to produce imminent lawless action. Note
the all-important "and"; both prongs of the *Brandenburg* test must
be met to justify restricting speech.

As of 2020, the Supreme Court has never allowed regulation
of any speech under that test. Nonetheless, some imaginable
falsehoods would satisfy the test and would be regulable for that
reason. Moreover, the *Brandenburg* test does not apply to some categories of "low-value" speech, such as commercial advertising and
criminal solicitation. Perhaps we could modify the test to say that if
falsehoods are likely to produce, and intended to produce, imminent
harm, they can be regulated for that reason as well (even if we are
not speaking of illegal action). That seems eminently reasonable. Or
perhaps we could go a bit further and add that if falsehoods really
are likely to produce harm, they can be regulated even if the harm
is not imminent.

But suppose that imminent harm is what is required. Even if so,
many falsehoods should be regulable. If someone claims that coronavirus is a hoax, there is an immediate threat to public health. If
someone commits perjury—by saying, for example, that she saw a
defendant at the scene of a crime, when she saw no such thing—the

likelihood of an unjust conviction is immediately increased. If someone claims to be a government agent, and so induces some action or statement from someone, there is an immediate harm. If someone sells a product with a false claim that it cures some illness, there is an immediate risk that people will waste their money on it (and fail to take appropriate steps to address that illness). The law already prohibits all of these statements. In fact, many falsehoods that the law forbids create something like a clear and present danger of harm (if not of independently lawless action).

But it is difficult to say something like that about other false statements of fact, which are more innocuous. Consider, for example, a claim from one neighbor to another, that her dog—who is actually a mixed breed—is a pure-bred Labrador retriever, or an exaggerated report about an alleged achievement on the tennis court over the weekend. With the foregoing arguments in mind, we should be willing to agree that if false statements do not produce any real harm, they cannot be regulated.

It is important to emphasize that many falsehoods can be harmful even if it cannot be said that they create a clear and present danger. The danger might not be "clear," in the sense that it might not be more likely than not, and it might not be "present," in the sense that it might not be imminent. In Chapter 2, I suggested that in principle, what matters is the expected value of the harm, that is, its probability multiplied by its magnitude. If a falsehood is 40 percent likely to create a catastrophe, the argument for regulating it is stronger than if it is 80 percent likely to create something a little bit bad. A harm tomorrow might be worse than a harm in a year, but a harm in a year should not be ignored. A sensible government does not ignore a small risk of catastrophe in five years.

These points bear directly on real-world cases. Holocaust denials might fuel anti-Semitism, even if not imminently. Claims about US responsibility for the 9/11 attacks can discredit efforts to counteract terrorism, even if not imminently. False claims about presidents and presidential candidates can be delegitimating or worse, even if we cannot say that they are likely to produce imminent harm. How should such cases be handled? With Mill's concerns and the foregoing points in mind, we might propose the following principle:

> *False statements are constitutionally protected unless the government can show that they threaten to cause serious harm that cannot be avoided through a more speech-protective route.*

That principle seems reasonable, and it is hard to see how any simple alternative could be better. In the real world, the principle is certainly a sensible place to start—not only for governments, but also for television stations, newspapers, and social media providers such as Facebook and Twitter. To be sure, it does not answer some important questions. Does it cover lies, or should they be given less protection than mere mistakes? What, exactly, is meant by the phrase, "threaten to cause serious harm"?

I will return to these points in the context of concrete cases. But before we get there, let us now turn to the question of how beliefs are formed.

CHAPTER SIX

Falsehoods Fly

WHY DO PEOPLE credit falsehoods? Why don't they dismiss them? Here is a large part of the answer: Most of the time, we believe other people. When they tell us things, we assume that they are telling the truth. To be sure, we consider some people untrustworthy, perhaps because they have so proved themselves, perhaps because they belong to a group that we think we should distrust. But on average, we trust people even when we should not. We pay too little attention to clear evidence that what is being said is false. We fail to discount for the circumstances.

TRUTH BIAS

A general phenomenon goes by the name of "truth bias":[1] People tend to think that what they hear is truthful, even if they have excellent reason not to believe what they hear. If people are provided with information that has clearly been discredited, they might nonetheless rely on that information in forming their judgments. Similarly, people are more likely to misremember, as true, a statement that they have been explicitly told is false than to misremember, as false, a statement that they have been explicitly told is true.

It follows that if you are told that some public official is a liar and a crook, you might continue to believe that, in some part of your mind, even if you know that she's perfectly honest. (In 2016, the sustained attacks on Hillary Clinton worked for this reason, even when people were aware that they were lies.) And if you are told that if you're under the age of fifty, you really don't need to worry about a pandemic, you might hold onto that belief, at least in some part of your mind, even after you are informed that people under fifty can get really sick.

The underlying problem goes by an unlovely name: "meta-cognitive myopia."[2] The basic idea is that we are highly attuned to "primary information": whether the weather report says that it is going to be cold today, whether a candidate for public office claims that he was a war hero, whether the local newspaper reports that a famous television star committed a drug offense. By contrast, we are far less attuned to "meta-information," meaning information about whether primary information is accurate. If you are given a clear signal that the supposed weather report was a joke, or that a public official is distorting his record in order to attract votes, you won't exactly ignore the signal. But if you're like most people, you will give it less weight than you should.

Evolutionary explanations are often speculative, but there is a reasonable one for truth bias. In hunter-gatherer societies, survival often depends on how people react to the evidence of their own senses, or even to signals that they receive from others. If you see a tiger chasing you, you had better run. And if your friends and neighbors are running, it makes sense to run too. There is much less urgency to picking up on signals about whether signals are reliable. To be sure, meta-cognition can be valuable, but primary information is the most important. That is enough to produce truth bias.

For a powerful demonstration of the existence of truth bias, consider some work from a research team consisting of Oxford's Myrto Pantazi, and Olivier Klein and Mikhail Kissine, both of the Free University of Brussels.[3] To simplify a complex story, Pantazi and his colleagues gave a large number of participants information involving criminal defendants in two legal cases. Participants were explicitly told that some of the information that they received, bearing on the appropriate sentence, was false. They were asked to come up with an appropriate prison term and also to say how dangerous the defendant was. The main question was whether people would adequately discount information that they were told was false, so that it would not influence their judgments.

The answer is that they did not. When people received negative information about the defendant, they were influenced by it, even when they had been explicitly informed that it was not true. As the authors put it, "jurors may judge defendants based on evidence that they encounter, even if they clearly know this evidence to be false." Consistent with other research, the authors also found that their participants tended to misremember false evidence as being true—and did so more often than they remembered true evidence as being false.

Pantazi and his colleagues undertook the same experiment with professional judges. Amazingly, they obtained the same basic results. Even if you are an experienced judge, false information about a criminal defendant might well affect your conclusions—and you might well remember it as true. Negative information in particular puts a kind of stamp in the human mind, and removing it is not easy.

These experiments involve law, but the lesson is much larger. Suppose you are in a new town and you ask strangers for directions. You will probably assume that they are telling you the truth, rather than trying to get you lost. In fact it might take a great deal to convince you that they were lying. In most settings, most of us assume that other members of the human species are telling the truth. That is our default assumption. That is one reason, by the way, that advertising works, even if we should know better than to believe it.

As noted, there are times and places in which we do not indulge that assumption. We know that some people are liars. If we think that people care only about themselves and not about us, we are far less likely to believe them. We do not think that the statements of advertisers have the same credibility as the statements of our best friends. But if we read something online or in a newspaper, we often ignore, or give too little weight to, clear signals that it is false.

FALSEHOODS SPREAD FASTER THAN TRUTH

It might be tempting at this point to emphasize that in many of the situations that most concern us, falsehoods will be met by truth. As we have seen, that is one of the cornerstones of the argument for protecting lies; the word "counterspeech" often operates as a kind of trump card in relevant debates. The Supreme Court plays that card, and so do social media platforms. But evidence suggests that by every measure, falsehoods are more likely to spread than truth. That does not mean that truth does not win out. But for those who believe in the marketplace of ideas and democratic self-government, it is a serious problem.

A relevant study, conducted by Soroush Vosoughi, Deb Roy, and Sinan Aral of the Massachusetts Institute of Technology, was based on a massive data set, consisting of all fact-checked rumor "cascades" that spread on Twitter from 2006 to 2017.[4] All in all, there were about 126,000 such cascades, spread by about 3 million people more than 4.5 million times.

To test whether truth was stronger than falsehood, the researchers looked at rumors that had been fact-checked by six independent organizations (Snopes.com, PolitiFact.com, FactCheck.org, TruthOrFiction.com, Hoax-Slayer.com, and UrbanLegendsOnline. com). The different organizations reached the same conclusion about these rumors at least 95 percent of the time. Using careful statistical tests, Vosoughi and his co-authors found that "falsehood diffused significantly farther, faster, deeper, and more broadly than the truth in all categories of information." For example, falsehoods reached 1,500 people six times more rapidly than truth. And while false statements about business, science, and entertainment did better than true ones, the biggest difference was in the domain of politics. Importantly, the researchers found that falsehoods do not spread only or mostly because of the actions of "bots." Vosoughi and his co-authors re-ran their study while using a bot-detection algorithm to identify and remove all bots—and they found that all of their main conclusions held. Human beings, it seems, are far more likely to spread falsehood than truth.

As Vosoughi and his co-authors speculate, one reason may be novelty. It is reasonable to hypothesize that novel information is more likely to spread, and that hypothesis may help to explain the comparative popularity of falsehoods. Enlisting a variety of metrics to test whether tweets convey new information, they find that "false rumors were measurably more novel than true rumors." Psychologists have also found that rumors are more likely to spread if they produce identifiable emotions, such as disgust.[5] Vosoughi and his co-authors compared the emotional content of replies to true and false rumors. They found that truth produced greater sadness, trust, and anticipation— while falsehoods produced greater surprise and disgust.

These are striking and important findings, but it is possible to raise some questions. Vosoughi and his colleagues do not quite show that falsehoods are more likely to spread than truth. More precisely, they find that within the category of popular rumors tested by independent fact-finding bodies, the false ones are especially likely to spread. But independent fact-checkers investigate only a very small subset of both false and true statements. Of that subset, the false ones may be especially provocative and interesting, above all in the political domain. Anticipating this objection, Vosoughi and his co-authors also had their students study a sample of rumor cascades that had not been verified by fact-finding organizations. Their central conclusion held: Rumors found to be false spread more quickly than rumors found to be true.

Much more remains to be learned about which falsehoods are most likely to spread, and also about why and when falsehoods spread more quickly than truth, and (most important) which, of the many falsehoods that spread, people are most likely to believe (and which people are most likely to believe them). By itself, the fact that falsehoods spread does not mean that they are influential; they might be received as fiction (or as a horror movie). It is clear, however, that falsehoods are often arresting and vivid, because they are novel and interesting, and more likely to disrupt expectations. It is also clear that when falsehoods trigger certain emotional reactions, including indignation and disgust, numerous people might end up hearing about them in a short time. Significantly, these points interact in troubling ways with truth bias: If falsehoods are especially likely to spread, and if people are biased in the direction of thinking that what they hear is true, then the risk that people will believe falsehoods increases dramatically. That is a serious problem for Mill's understanding of why it is important to protect falsehoods.

DO CORRECTIONS WORK?

It is natural to respond that so long as speech is free, falsehoods can always be corrected, even if they spread. But do corrections work?

A great deal of evidence suggests that the answer is not a simple "yes." Sometimes corrections do work. But sometimes corrections fail; they have no effect at all. And sometimes corrections backfire; they intensify people's commitment to their original erroneous belief.

An influential study, conducted by political scientist Brendan Nyhan of Dartmouth College and two co-authors, helps explain why.[6] One group of participants was provided with a 2009 news article in which former Alaska governor Sarah Palin claimed that the Affordable Care Act created "death panels" and that these panels included bureaucrats authorized to decide whether seniors were "worthy of health care." A separate group was given the same news story, but with an appended correction saying that "nonpartisan health care experts have concluded that Palin is wrong." The study's central question: Would the correction have any effect? Would people who saw the correction be less likely to believe that the Affordable Care Act calls for death panels?

Not surprisingly, the correction was more likely to convince people who viewed Palin unfavorably than those who had a high opinion of her. Notably, the correction also tended to sway the participants who liked Palin but who did not have a lot of political knowledge (as measured by their answers to general questions, such as how many terms a president may serve).

Here is the most interesting finding in the study. Those who viewed Palin favorably, and who also had a lot of political knowledge, were not persuaded by the correction. On the contrary, it made them more likely to believe Palin was right. While the correction tended to convince Palin supporters who lacked political knowledge that she was wrong about death panels, it generally failed to persuade Palin supporters who had such knowledge. For those supporters, the correction actually backfired.

There are two explanations. The first is that if you know a lot about politics, you are more likely to be emotionally invested in what you believe. Efforts to undermine or dislodge those beliefs might well anger or upset you and therefore backfire. When beliefs are motivated, it is hard to dislodge them, and efforts may be counterproductive. The second explanation is that if you have a lot of political knowledge, you are more likely to think that you know what is really true, which means it will be pretty hard for people to convince you otherwise. If anything, a supposed correction might make you suspicious. Why would someone bother to deny it, if it weren't true? The general lesson is both straightforward and disturbing. People who know a great deal, and who distrust a particular messenger, might well be impervious to factual corrections, even if what they believe turns out to be false. The effect of corrections might be to fortify their initial beliefs.

It is important to emphasize that the backfire effect is hardly universal.[7] If people think that there are 183 nations in the United Nations, and then are told that the actual number is 193, they are likely to shift their views. If people think that India has a larger population than China, and then hear that China has the world's largest population, they will learn from what they hear. If people think that Frankfurt is the capital of Germany, and then read that it is Berlin, they will not insist with new fervor that it is Frankfurt. It matters whether they begin with what they consider to be very good reasons for their original view. It also matters whether they have a strong emotional commitment to that view—whether they like maintaining it and dislike losing it. It matters, finally, whether the source is deemed to be credible.

A general lesson is that for a very wide range of factual questions, corrections from credible sources will indeed work. But for an important subset of questions, potentially involving public health or democracy itself, belief in false statements might persist. For that reason, falsehoods can have a long-term effect, even if they appear to have been corrected.

LEARNING FROM OTHERS

"Who are you gonna believe? Me, or your lying eyes?" The famous question, often attributed to Groucho Marx, signals the power of social influences. Your eyes are unlikely to be lying. But maybe you can be convinced to think so. In the most vivid work, conducted by Solomon Asch, individuals were apparently willing to abandon the direct evidence of their own senses.[8] They embraced palpable falsehoods. In a sense, they were willing to accept fake news. They did not believe their lying eyes, or at least they said that they didn't.[9]

In Asch's classic experiments, a line of a certain length was placed on a large white card. The task of the subjects was to "match" that line by choosing, as identical to it in length, one of three other lines, placed on a separate large white card. One of the lines on the second white card was in fact identical in length to the line to be matched to it; the other two were substantially different, with the differential varying from an inch and three quarters to three quarters of an inch. The subject in the original experiments was one of eight people asked to engage in the matching. But unbeknownst to that subject, the other people apparently being tested were actually there as Asch's confederates, serving as part of the experiments.

These experiments unfolded in the following way. In the first two rounds, everyone agreed about the right answer; this seemed to be an extremely dull experiment. But the third round introduced "an unexpected disturbance."[10] Other group members made what was obviously, to the subject and to any reasonable person, a clear error; they matched the line at issue to one that was obviously longer or shorter. In these circumstances, the subject had the choice of maintaining his independent judgment or instead yielding to the crowd. A large number of people ended up yielding. In ordinary circumstances, subjects erred less than 1 percent of the time; but when other members of the group gave a wrong answer, subjects erred 36.8% of the time. Indeed, in a series of twelve questions, no less than 70% of subjects went along with the group, and defied the evidence of their own senses, at least once. They heard a false statement of fact—and they were willing to agree with it in a public setting.

Other studies have identified an important feature of conformity, directly bearing on the spread of falsehoods: much depends on the subject's perceived relationship to the experimenters' confederates and in particular *on whether the subject considers himself part of the same group in which those confederates fall.* Thus conformity—and hence error—is dramatically *increased*, in public statements, when the subject perceives himself as part of a reasonably discrete group that includes the experimenter's confederates (all Catholics or all Democrats, for example).[11]

By contrast, conformity is dramatically *decreased*, and hence error is also dramatically decreased, in public statements. when the subject perceives himself as in a different group from the experimenter's confederates (all Episcopalians or all Republicans, for example).[12] Notably, private opinions, expressed anonymously afterward, did not differ, depending on whether the subject perceived himself as a member of the same group as others in the experiment.

Why do people sometimes ignore the evidence of their own senses? Why do they embrace a clear falsehood? The two principal explanations point to information and peer pressure. Some of Asch's subjects seem to have thought that the unanimous group members must be right. They believed that, for some reason, their own eyes were lying. In Asch's studies, many conformists said, in private interviews, that their own opinions must have been wrong—a point that suggests that information, rather than peer pressure, is what was moving them. This informational account is strengthened by a study in which people who recorded their answers anonymously gave nearly as many wrong answers as they had under Asch's own conditions—suggesting that they really believed what they were saying.[13] A similar study found that conformity is not lower when the subject's response is unavailable to the majority.[14]

But some people did respond to peer pressure. Asch's subjects included people who were clear on the truth but who were unwilling to make, in public, what others would see as an error. Experimenters generally find significantly reduced error, in the same basic circumstances as Asch's experiments, when subjects are asked to give a purely private answer. In the same vein, experiments find higher levels of conformity when it is very easy for everyone to see whether people are conforming or deviating.[15]

Whether people sincerely believe that falsehoods are true or are simply unwilling to defy the group, Asch concluded that his results suggest "the social process is polluted" by the "dominance of conformity."[16] He added, "That we have found the tendency to conformity in our society so strong that reasonably intelligent and well-meaning young people are willing to call white black is a matter of concern."[17] Conformity plays a major role in the spread of lies and errors. People rely on what others say, even if they have excellent reason to believe that it is not true.

CASCADES

Some of the most interesting recent work on the spread of falsehoods points to the importance of social cascades.[18] The starting point here is that when people lack much in the way of private information (and sometimes even when they have such information), they rely on information provided by the statements or actions of others.

Consider a stylized example, involving four people in a close-knit group. Suppose that Barbara has no idea whether genetically modified food poses a public health risk, but that her friend Adam says (wrongly) that it does. If she trusts Adam, she might well be persuaded by his conviction. If Adam and Barbara both believe that genetically modified food poses a public health risk, Catherine may end up thinking that too, at least if she lacks reliable independent information to the contrary. If Adam, Barbara, and Catherine believe that genetically modified food poses a public health risk, David will have to have a good deal of confidence to reject their shared conclusion.

People typically have different "thresholds" before they will believe something that turns out to be false. As those with low thresholds come to a certain belief or action, people with somewhat higher thresholds will join them, possibly to a point where a critical mass is reached, making groups, organizations, communities, political parties, and possibly even nations "tip."[19] The result of this process can be to produce snowball or cascade effects, as small or even large groups of people end up believing something that is false, simply because other people seem to believe that it is true. There is a great deal of experimental evidence of informational cascades, which are easy to induce in the laboratory;[20] falsehoods often spread as a result of cascade effects.

Thus far the discussion has involved purely informational pressures and informational cascades, where people care about what other people think because they do not know what to think, and they rely on the opinions of others. But there can be reputational pressures and reputational cascades as well.[21] Here the basic idea is that people speak out, or remain silent, or even act largely in order to preserve their reputations, even at the price of failing to say what they really think. False beliefs can arise and entrench themselves in this way.

Suppose, for example, that Allen believes that climate change does not pose a serious problem; suppose too that Barbara thinks that Allen is full of nonsense. Barbara may keep quiet, or (like some of Asch's subjects) even agree with Allen, simply to preserve Allen's good opinion. Charles may see that Allen believes that climate change does not pose a serious problem, and that Barbara seems to agree with Allen; Charles may therefore voice agreement with the two of them even though privately he is skeptical or ambivalent.

It is easy to see how this kind of thing might happen in political life, with politicians expressing their commitment to some factual statement (including that climate change is not real), simply to avoid the reputational damage. (Under the presidency of Donald Trump, many Republican politicians, privately skeptical of Trump, participated in a reputational cascade.) People will typically have different thresholds before they will yield to the views of others. Some people will yield to perceived pressure only when it is very severe (for example, because a large number of people impose it), whereas others will yield when it is mild (for example, simply because a few trusted others impose it). Here too the consequence can be cascade effects—large social movements in one direction or another—as increasing numbers of people yield to a pressure that they simultaneously impose, eventually reaching a critical mass. At that stage, a large number of people eventually appear to support a certain belief or course of action simply because others (appear to) do so. Widespread support for falsehoods can arise in this way. Recall Hans Christian Andersen's tale of the Emperor's New Clothes, which is memorable because it tells us something true and important about human societies.

Sometimes cascades are quite fragile. The reason is that people's statements and actions are not based on clear convictions. People can believe that a politician is a crook or that a vaccine is dangerous—but shift quickly. That is good news. The problem is that social cascades, both informational and reputational, can lead to widespread factual errors. Numerous people can end up seeming to believe, or actually believing, something that is not true. That is a real problem for the view that false statements of fact will be fixed by the marketplace of ideas.

GROUP POLARIZATION

Suppose that a group of ten people tends to believe that something is true, even though it is not. They might believe that some public official has done something terribly wrong or that some product does or does not cause a public health risk. What will happen after they speak with one another? The likely answer is that they will become more confident, more unified, and more extreme in their commitment to their false belief. The phenomenon is known as group polarization. As James Madison put it, "The reason of man, like man himself, is timid and cautious when left alone, and acquires firmness and confidence in proportion to the number with which it is associated."[22]

Group polarization is among the most robust patterns found in deliberating bodies, and it has been found in many places. Polarization occurs when group discussion leads group members to a more extreme point in line with their tendencies before they started to talk.[23] Consider some examples of the basic phenomenon, which has been found in over a dozen nations.[24]

(a) A group of moderately profeminist women will become more strongly profeminist after discussion.[25]

(b) After discussion, citizens of France become more critical of the United States and its intentions with respect to economic aid.[26]

(c) After discussion, whites predisposed to show racial prejudice offer more negative responses to the question of whether white racism is responsible for conditions faced by African Americans in American cities.[27]

(d) After discussion, whites predisposed not to show racial prejudice offer more positive responses to the same question.[28]

As statistical regularities, it should follow, for example, that those who believe that climate change is a serious problem are likely, after discussion, to hold that belief with considerable confidence; that people who believe that some actions will not reduce the spread of COVID-19 will become more entrenched in that belief after internal discussions; that people who believe that some public figure has committed a terrible crime will become more unified and more intensely committed to that belief as a result of their discussions with one another.

The phenomenon of group polarization has conspicuous importance to the spread of falsehoods online, where groups with distinctive identities often engage in within-group discussion. (Those identities might be political, ethnic, religious, or ideological; they might involve some random social connection that assumes salience.) If the public is balkanized, and if different groups design their own preferred communications packages, the consequence may be further balkanization with respect to facts, as group members move one another toward more extreme points in line with their initial tendencies. Different deliberating groups, each consisting of like-minded people, may be driven increasingly far apart, simply because most of their discussions are with one another. On questions of fact, members of a political party, or of the

principal political parties, may polarize as a result of internal discussions; party-line voting is sometimes explicable partly on this
ground. Extremist groups will often become more extreme; the
largest group polarization typically occurs with individuals already
inclined toward extremes. And when their extremism is a product
of false beliefs, there are multiple dangers.

What can be done, in a system committed to freedom of speech?

CHAPTER SEVEN

Your Good Name

SUPPOSE THAT IN a few years, a US senator named Pamela Wilson decides to run for the presidency. Suppose that Wilson is subject to a vicious smear campaign. She is accused of having been an alcoholic; of cheating in college; of having said, behind closed doors, that she hates the United States and wants to destroy its military. All of these accusations are false. Some of them have been spread by people who know that they are untrue. Some have been spread by people who did not exactly know that—but who should have. If we believe in free speech, do we think that Wilson should be able to stop the lies? To seek damages? Should public officials be allowed to intervene? How?

Many nations attempt to balance the interest in reputation with the interest in free speech. A person whose reputation has been harmed can often invoke the law of defamation, defined to include libel for written statements and slander for oral statements. In the United States, the law differs from state to state, but in a standard formulation, the plaintiff must allege (1) that the defendant has made a false and defamatory statement of fact; (2) that the statement was made "of and concerning" the plaintiff; (3) that the statement was published or shown to a third party; and (4) that the statement caused injury to the plaintiff. A statement is defamatory if it could damage the plaintiff's reputation in the community—for example, because it tends to expose the plaintiff to public contempt, hatred, ridicule, aversion, or disgrace. In the United States, unlike in England, truth has usually been a defense to a defamation action. But to be subject to such an action, the defendant need not have known that the statement was false. In many states, the mere fact of falsity would be enough.

Defamation law serves two critical purposes. First, it deters harmful and possibly horrific misconduct. If someone is tempted to try to destroy someone—because of personal animus, a commercial goal, a feeling of hurt, or a political or ideological mission—the possibility of a defamation action is meant to create a powerful disincentive. And if a speaker or writer does not aim to destroy someone but is simply reckless, negligent, or mistaken, defamation law insists: *Proceed at your own risk.* Second, defamation law gives injured people a chance both to obtain compensation and to clear their names. If deterrence does not work, defamation law gives people an after-the-fact chance to make things right, or at least closer to right.

The stakes here can be very high. A defamatory remark can impose devastating economic and personal harm on people. It can even ruin their lives. To say the least, a claim that you are a drug addict, that you have assaulted a child, or that you have betrayed your country is no light matter. And such a claim can have harmful effects not only on its direct victims but also on friends and family members and even private and public institutions. If a company's head is defamed, the company itself may be badly hurt. And if a mayor or a governor is defamed, the harmful effects will ripple through democracy itself.

When lawyers and judges discuss how to achieve the proper balance, they usually speak of, and deplore, the chilling effect that is created by the prospect of civil or criminal penalties for any kind of speech. Fearing the threat of damage actions, penalties, and lawsuits, whistleblowers, experts, journalists, and bloggers might keep their opinions to themselves.[1] A legal system ought not to discourage questions, objections, and dissent, which can promote accountability and uncover error or corruption. Strict rules of defamation law can chill speech about public figures and public issues in a way that could damage democratic debate. Back to Mill: To the degree that there is anything like a marketplace of ideas, we should be especially concerned about the chilling effect, because it will undermine processes that ultimately produce the truth.

But again, let us avoid an emphasis on only one side of the equation. We have seen that for increasingly clear reasons, the marketplace of ideas can fail, ensuring that false statements will spread and become entrenched. Recall a point of special importance to defamation: People often engage in "motivated reasoning"; they credit false statements because they *like* believing that they are true.[2] Under certain conditions, correcting defamatory falsehoods can be exceptionally difficult. We have also seen that the chilling effect should often be welcomed, especially if it comes from social norms that encourage truth telling and discourage inaccurate statements of all kinds (including lies).

We have also seen that some falsehoods are not harmful, or not only harmful. They help people to understand the truth, at least in the long run. But many falsehoods are not merely damaging but also entirely useless to those who seek to know what is true. A society without any chilling effect, imposed by social norms and by law, would be a singularly ugly place. What societies need is not the absence of "chill," but an optimal level. This conclusion bears in particular on the law of defamation. The question is: How do we get there?

ONCE UPON A TIME

From 1791, when the Bill of Rights was ratified, through 1963, the Supreme Court never ruled that the First Amendment imposed serious limits on the use of defamation law. States were allowed to act essentially as they wished. The basic idea was that the Constitution's protection of "the freedom of speech" did not include certain categories of communication. Those categories were not included in the term. Some modern readers find this puzzling. Isn't "the freedom of speech" an absolute, by the plain language of the Constitution? Beware of this conclusion. The First Amendment says this, in relevant part: "Congress shall make no law . . . abridging the freedom of speech, or of the press." Those who ratified this provision might well have understood "the freedom of speech" to include some kinds of communications, and not others. They might well have thought that some restrictions on some communications did not "abridge" that form of freedom. In fact that is certainly true.[3]

Until 1978, commercial speech was not protected, even if it was truthful, and certainly if it was not. (It is now protected, but not if it is false.) Obscene speech was not protected, though there were disputes about the size of the category. As we have seen, falsehoods were generally said to lack constitutional protection. Because the common law had long regulated defamatory speech, and because the longstanding understanding was that such regulation was not forbidden by the First Amendment, the Constitution was not taken to create a problem.

Everything changed as a result of the famous case of *New York Times Co. v. Sullivan*, which must be counted as one of the most important (and also radical) in the history of the US Supreme Court.[4] The decision itself may be familiar, but with recent objections in mind,[5] it will be useful to approach it anew, to understand the context, and to see what the Court actually said. The ruling, now taken for granted by so many, was very much a product of its time—and it was anything but foreordained. We should be able to imagine, with relative ease, a world without *New York Times v. Sullivan*. Whether that would be a better world is a fair question to ask.

For present purposes, the bare facts of the case were simple. In the early 1960s, civil rights organizations ran an advertisement in the *New York Times*, in which they complained of brutal police responses to civil rights protests in Montgomery, Alabama. For example, the third paragraph said this:

> In Montgomery, Alabama, after students sang "My Country, 'Tis of Thee" on the State Capitol steps, their leaders were expelled from school, and truckloads of police armed with shotguns and tear-gas ringed the Alabama State College Campus. When the entire student body protested to state authorities by refusing to reregister, their dining hall was padlocked in an attempt to starve them into submission.

The advertisement was signed at the bottom of the page by the "Committee to Defend Martin Luther King and the Struggle for Freedom in the South."

L. B. Sullivan, the Montgomery commissioner who supervised the police, brought suit for libel. He was not mentioned by name, but he contended that the word "police" clearly referred to him, that he was being accused of "ringing" the campus with police, and that he was being blamed for padlocking the dining hall in order to starve the students into submission. It was not disputed that the advertisement contained falsehoods. For example, the campus dining hall was not padlocked on any occasion, and while the police were deployed near the campus, they did not at any time "ring" the campus.

There is also no question that the case was a civil rights case, not only a case about freedom of expression. In important respects, the libel action was directed against the civil rights movement.[6] It was an effort to make some kind of public statement and to exact some kind of revenge. And it worked. After deliberating for less than three hours, the jury awarded Sullivan the precise amount that he wanted, a whopping $500,000 (about $4.2 million in 2020 dollars).

Under Alabama law at the time, a publication counted as "libelous *per se*" if the words "tend to injure a person . . . in his reputation" or to "bring [him] into public contempt." In the *New York Times v. Sullivan* litigation itself, the Alabama trial court said that this standard would be met if the words were such as to injure Sullivan "in his public office, or impute misconduct to him in his office, or want of official integrity, or want of fidelity to a public trust."

The US Supreme Court said that this standard was unconstitutional, even as applied to falsehoods. It ruled that when a public official is involved, the Constitution allows recovery only if the speaker has "actual malice." This means that speakers cannot be held liable unless (a) they were actually aware that the statement was false or (b) they acted "with reckless disregard" for the question of truth or falsity. The idea of actual awareness is straightforward in principle ("did you know you weren't telling the truth?"), though it might be hard to prove in individual cases. The idea of reckless disregard is a bit trickier; recall the taxonomy in Chapter 2. If it is quite obvious that a statement is false, and a reporter publishes it even so, the Constitution allows the victim to sue.[7] But in general, the actual malice standard is highly protective of people who spread falsehoods. The puzzle here is that while the Court said repeatedly, during this period, that false statements as such do not have First

Amendment value, the Court was nonetheless providing a great deal of protection to those very statements.

In explaining its conclusions, the Court stressed that the First Amendment limits the power of public officials and courts, even when the goal is to control libelous statements. Seeming to echo Mill, and to rely on arguments akin to those outlined in Chapter 5, the Court said that "erroneous statement is inevitable in free debate, and . . . it must be protected if the freedoms of expressions are to have the 'breathing space' that they 'need . . . to survive.'"[8] Thus neither "factual error" nor "defamatory content" would be enough to remove the constitutional protection accorded to "criticism of official conduct."[9] The Court emphasized that the free speech principle broadly protects speech that bears on public affairs.

For public officials, the Court ruled two approaches out of bounds. It said that "strict liability"—meaning liability without fault—is constitutionally unacceptable. Under the First Amendment, speakers cannot be held liable simply because they spread falsehoods. The Court also protected journalists and others who acted unreasonably (and thus were negligent and therefore liable under long-standing law). That ruling cut out the heart from much of the law of defamation. Imagine that a falsehood, published in the *New York Post*, seriously injures a public official and that the author and the editor really should have known (in light of the evidence they had) that the statement was false. Even if so, the author, the editor, and the *Post* are free from liability so long as they did not know that the statement was false and so long as they were not "recklessly indifferent" to the question of truth or falsity. The result is to create a lot of breathing room for people who spread falsehoods.

Because *New York Times Co. v. Sullivan* involved public officials, it left some key questions open. What if someone libels a private individual, someone who lacks fame or notoriety? What if a newspaper publishes some damaging falsehood about an ordinary person named Joe Smith, accusing him of corruption, bribery, theft, or other misconduct? Under long-standing principles in Anglo-American law, Smith may recover damages, and he need not even establish fault.[10] The very facts of falsehood and harm are enough to give Smith a right to sue. The Court's analysis in *New York Times Co. v. Sullivan*, focusing on the risk of chilling effect and the need for breathing space in the context of "criticism of official conduct," did not by itself raise doubts about Smith's ability to invoke the courts to protect his reputation.

Nonetheless, the Court eventually concluded that the free speech principle imposes restrictions on Smith's libel action too—a conclusion that has implications for what is being said every day on television, Facebook, Twitter, YouTube, and anywhere else. In *Gertz v. Robert Welch, Inc.*,[11] the Court ruled that ordinary people could recover damages for libel only if they could prove negligence. What this means is that if someone says something false and damaging, it is not enough that the statement was false and that the subject was badly harmed. The subject must also show that the speaker did not exercise proper care.

While it is exceedingly difficult to prove "actual malice," it is not exactly easy to establish negligence. Suppose that a reporter learns, from an apparently credible source, that a lawyer or a banker has engaged in some corrupt conduct, or that a high school teacher was sexually involved with a student, or that a candidate for public office lied in some public document. Suppose that the allegation is false. Perhaps the reporter can be deemed negligent for failing to ensure that his source was right or for failing to ask alternative sources. But perhaps not. It will not be easy for people to demonstrate that the reporter was negligent as a matter of law.

To explain its conclusion in *Gertz*, the Court again invoked the idea of chilling effect and announced that free speech "requires that we protect some falsehood in order to protect speech that matters."[12]

In *New York Times Co. v. Sullivan*, after all, the Court had said that a "defense for erroneous statements honestly made" is "essential."[13] According to the Court, what was said there applies in *Gertz* as well: "A rule compelling the critic . . . to guarantee the truth of all his factual assertions—and to do so on pain of libel judgments virtually unlimited in amount—leads to . . . 'self-censorship.' "[14] A constitutional ban on liability without fault, along with a requirement that negligence be shown, operates as a safeguard against journalistic or speaker self-silencing. In short, the Court continued the enterprise, started in *New York Times Co. v. Sullivan*, of attempting to regulate the extent of the "chill" on free speech.

In *Alvarez*, the plurality similarly emphasized that false statements of fact are sometimes protected in order to prevent the chilling effect: "Some false statements are inevitable if there is to be an open and vigorous expression of views in public and private conversation, expression the First Amendment seeks to guarantee."[15] In some sense, that is true. But the question remains: How many false statements are optimal? How many are too many? A billion? Every day?

FOUNDATIONS

Constitutional limits on libel law can be assessed from many different directions. The first question, of course, is the choice of method: How should a Constitution be interpreted? We have seen that some people are "originalists"; they believe that the Constitution should be interpreted in accordance with its "original public meaning." For originalists, the Constitution means what it meant at the time that it was ratified. Notwithstanding a brief historical discussion, *New York Times Co. v. Sullivan* was not much grounded in the original public meaning of the First Amendment. If we are originalists, the decision is exceedingly difficult to defend.[16] For the founding generation, it was perfectly acceptable to allow broad use of the law of defamation, to allow people to protect their reputations. Justice Clarence Thomas writes in no uncertain terms:[17]

> The constitutional libel rules adopted by this Court in *New York Times* and its progeny broke sharply from the common law of libel, and there are sound reasons to question whether the First and Fourteenth Amendments displaced this body of common law. . . . Far from increasing a public figure's burden in a defamation action, the common law deemed libels against public figures to be, if anything, more serious and injurious than ordinary libels. . . . The Court consistently listed libel among the "well-defined and narrowly limited classes of speech, the prevention and punishment of which have never been thought to raise any Constitutional problem." . . . There are sound reasons to question whether either the First or Fourteenth Amendment, as originally understood, encompasses an actual-malice standard for public figures or otherwise displaces vast swaths of state defamation law.

On this count, Justice Thomas might well be right, though early debates over the constitutionality of the Sedition Act of 1798, briefly discussed in *New York Times* itself, raise some questions. But most justices are not originalists, and instead of embracing originalism, the *New York Times* decision seems rooted in a more pragmatic approach, taking the First Amendment to set out a general principle, and assuming that the Court's role is to see how that principle is best understood, given contemporary values and the competing interests. That understanding of the Court's role is of course contested. But for the sake of simplicity, and without taking a stand on the contested issues, let us explore the issue in the broadly pragmatic terms generally used in the Court's free speech opinions.

A central point in *New York Times Co. v. Sullivan*, and a continuing concern for the modern era, involves an appreciation of two problems: political bias and official power. Either of these is dangerous in itself; the two can be a potent combination. Suppose, for example, that President Donald Trump's attorney general, William Barr, is bringing suit against a newspaper, contending that it has libeled the president (or otherwise violated some law). Suppose Trump directed Barr to bring the suit. Suppose too that in doing that, Trump was not exactly objective. He was attempting to punish the newspaper for carrying a story that cast him in a bad light. He was also attempting to deter other newspapers from doing that. The very fact of the lawsuit might deter negative coverage of the president. With this hypothetical, we are getting uncomfortably close to authoritarianism.

Political bias can be found whenever a prosecutor, a judge, a jury, or even a well-funded private plaintiff is acting in order to deter and punish speech that takes a certain stand. Official power might be exercised by prosecutors not in a neutral effort to protect people's reputations but in an effort to respond to political interests or the will of a particular person or institution. It is important to emphasize the dangers posed by well-funded or ideological plaintiffs. Whether they win or not, they can essentially destroy the economic security of individuals and institutions, including news organizations. The mere requirement of mounting a defense usually imposes high costs, and they are not merely economic. We can easily imagine judges or juries that would be sympathetic to one or another side in political debates. Strong constitutional safeguards against the use of libel law might be seen, in the 1960s or now, as a kind of prophylactic against these risks.

Even so, we need to make some distinctions. Some false statements involve public officials (Cabinet officials, governors, mayors). Others involve celebrities—actors or dancers or singers—who are not connected to the government in any way. Still others involve not public officials but public issues; suppose, for example, that an ordinary person is accused of attempting to bribe an important executive at a local bank. Still others involve *victims* of civil or criminal wrongdoing, such as assault or sexual harassment. For those who fall within each of these categories, the law is generally clear. Celebrities are treated the same as public officials. Public issues are not given any kind of special status; the question turns on the status of the person who is bringing suit. Public figures cannot recover for libel unless they can show actual malice. Ordinary people must show negligence.

It is not at all clear that these rules strike the right balance. Consider those involved in public life: because actual malice is so difficult to establish, good people are subject to real damage, and those who do the damage usually cannot be held accountable in any way. As we have seen, the problem is not restricted to those who are damaged; it extends to self-government itself, which suffers if citizens cannot make fair evaluations. Consider entertainers: those who have decided to act or to sing are at increased risk of public ridicule or even cruelty, even if they have absolutely no role in politics. Consider ordinary people: it is not easy to demonstrate negligence, and if people spread a false and damaging rumor, it will be difficult to hold them accountable. The problem is especially serious in light of what is said on social media. The question of compensation is less important than the question of deterrence. With the law as it now stands, most false statements simply cannot be deterred.

It is far from clear that this is good, or even acceptable, from the standpoint of either freedom of expression or individual autonomy. Suppose that speakers or writers are acting negligently. If so, is it so clear that they should be able to spread falsehoods about candidates for public office? On what assumptions? Do we really want to allow people to be able to spread negligent falsehoods about actors and actresses? Is it important to allow journalists to carry stories that are full of harmful and false statements about Taylor Swift, Christian Bale, and Julia Roberts? (Answer: No.)

True, famous people have a distinctive ability to reach large audiences and thus to correct errors, but among many viewers and readers, the truth will not prevail. As we have seen, falsehoods will linger in people's minds. It is not especially important to provide breathing space for damaging falsehoods about actors, musicians, and other entertainers. In any case, it is not clear that ordinary people should be unable to sue when they have been harmed by falsehoods. Any marketplace requires standards and ground rules; no market can operate as a free-for-all. In the United States, the current regulatory system for free speech—the current setting of "chill"—is not the one that we would or should choose for the Internet era.

FIVE IDEAS

It may or may not be too late to suggest a fundamental rethinking of basic principles. But it is hardly too late to adapt those principles to the modern era. It is worth reiterating that *New York Times Co. v. Sullivan* was decided in 1964, which might as well be a century ago, or maybe a millennium, in light of the massive technological advances that followed it. Spreading libelous or otherwise damaging statements is far easier today than ever before; so is correcting them. Because of technological changes, it would be a miracle if the ruling represented the best approach today to accommodate the relevant values. Part of the force of the argument from the chilling effect points to the expense of lawsuits, including high damage awards. (Recall that $500,000 award in *New York v. Sullivan* itself, back in 1964.) If the law could find ways to protect people against falsehoods without producing the potentially excessive deterrence that comes from costly lawsuits, we might be able to accommodate the conflicting interests. Consider, then, some modest ideas meant to do exactly that.

First: Warnings and disclosures could be used to inform people that what has been said is not true. On Facebook and Twitter, for example, a false statement about an actor, a politician, or a noncelebrity could be accompanied by a few words, as in "get the real facts," or "this is false." Those words could themselves be accompanied by a link to the website where people can find out the truth. A response of this sort would build on actual practices on some social media platforms, including Facebook and Twitter.

Second: Damage caps and schedules could do a great deal to promote free speech values while also ensuring a measure of deterrence. Suppose, for example, that libel awards were usually bounded at a specified level (at the extreme, $1). A very low limit would of course reduce the deterrent effect. But speakers have reputations to protect as well. If they are subject to any liability at all, and if it is determined that they did not tell the truth, their reputations will suffer. From the standpoint of the system of freedom of expression, speakers' concern for their reputations is not exactly a disaster; from the standpoint of ensuring against harms to individuals, it is an extremely good thing. A cap on damages, alongside liability to establish what is actually true, could work to leverage the speaker's concern for his reputation to good effect.

Third: There might be a general right to demand correction or retraction after a clear demonstration that a statement is both false and damaging—in other words, defamatory under traditional legal standards. If a newspaper, broadcaster, or social media platform refuses to provide a prominent correction or retraction after a reasonable period of time, it might be liable for at least modest or nominal damages.

Fourth: On the Internet in particular, people might be given a right to "notice and take down" when they can show that they have been defamed. Under this approach, modeled on the copyright provisions of the Digital Millennium Copyright Act,[18] website operators, and perhaps social media providers, would be obliged to take down statements that are shown to be libelous under traditional common law standards upon proper notice. Such an obligation would require an amendment of § 230,[19] which immunizes social media platforms from most forms of liability.[20] Some courts have upheld immunity for online platforms against claims that platforms have unreasonably delayed removing libelous posts.[21]

Fifth: On social media in particular, defamatory statements, generally protected by the First Amendment, could be downgraded so that they are less likely to circulate. For example, they might be displayed rarely or not prominently on Facebook's News Feed. This approach would build on Facebook's existing strategy for misinformation.

To be sure, these proposals raise fair questions. For example, social media platforms are not courts and they are hardly in the best position to judge what is libelous. It does not seem reasonable to ask Facebook, Twitter, or YouTube to engage in anything like adjudication. The simplest approach would be to say that if a statement has been held to be libelous by a competent tribunal, social media providers must take it down and will be held liable if they do not. The problem with this approach is that it would do too little; most victims of libel do not sue at all. The question is whether in very clear cases, where there really is no reasonable doubt, social media providers should also have an obligation to take material down. In principle, the answer is almost certainly yes. The only question is whether it is possible to administer such a system. The best answer is that when there is a will, there is a way.

It is also true that because of the nature of the Internet, notice and takedown cannot provide a complete solution. Once material is posted, it might effectively be there forever.[22] But if it is taken down, it will not be in quite so many places, and at least the victim of the defamatory statement will be able to say that it was taken down.

Before we embrace any of these proposals, we would, of course, be required to undertake some sustained analysis of their likely consequences. I sketch them not to offer a verdict or to endorse any of them in particular, but to signal some possible approaches that might protect the legitimate rights of speakers while offering safeguards not only to those whose reputations might be damaged by falsehoods but also to the many others who are harmed when they are misinformed about people, places, and things.

What about newspapers, magazines, and social media providers? What should they be doing voluntarily and entirely on their own? None of these is subject to the First Amendment, which applies only to government. There is a good argument that on notice, all of them should take down statements that would be libelous under traditional standards, even if no actual malice is involved. Why would that not be the appropriate (voluntary) practice? Facebook's Community Standards do not allow "bullying and harassment."[23] This is to the company's credit. Also to its credit, those standards do not permit "misinformation that contributes to the risk of imminent violence or physical harm." Why shouldn't those standards also be directed against libel? At least after a clear demonstration that a libel has actually been committed?

Let us not lose the forest for the trees. In the United States, at least, the current system does not adequately protect people's reputations. It trivializes their interest in their good name. To be sure, defamation law could be used so as to undermine the system of freedom of expression in a serious way. But we should be able to think of new ways to deter defamatory falsehoods without compromising that system. That project is urgent, not only to protect people who are being seriously hurt, but also to protect those who care about them, and also allies, customers, investors, and citizens who lose when they lose.

CHAPTER EIGHT

. . .

Harm

CONSIDER THE FOLLOWING statements: "Cigarettes do not cause cancer." "Paul McCartney died in 1971." "Vaccinations cause autism." "Taylor Swift has lung cancer." "Climate change is a hoax." "The best way to avoid heart disease is to eat plenty of sugar."

Libel is important, but it is a pretty limited category, and it does not come close to capturing the full set of problems introduced by falsehoods and lies. We have seen that false statements create risks to public health and safety. They endanger the operation of the criminal justice system. They might make it difficult to run the tax system. We have also seen many examples of cases in which the law punishes falsehoods, and to those cases, few people are raising constitutional objections.

Should lawmakers and regulators, concerned about truth, go beyond libel? Or does libel have some unique status, such that broader efforts to focus on falsehoods and lies would raise insuperable constitutional objections? Some people would like to answer "no" and "yes," respectively, to these questions. But there is good reason to hesitate before doing that. The easy answers are too easy. Hannah

Arendt's words remain relevant: "While probably no former time tolerated so many diverse opinions on religious or philosophical matters, factual truth, if it happens to oppose a given group's profit or pleasure, is greeted today with greater hostility than ever before."[1]

Recall too that the government, like social media providers, has a large number of tools, including not only punishment and fines but also warnings, disclosure, and other efforts to educate users about what is true. To those who are concerned about adverse effects on free speech, the less intrusive tools might be appealing. And to those who are concerned about harm, the less intrusive tools might seem both necessary and sufficient.

In this chapter, I explore an assortment of problems, including nondefamatory falsehoods in the context of politics and political campaigns, deepfakes and altered videos, and falsehoods that threaten public health. Many other falsehoods, and many other lies, cause serious dangers. My hope is that the problems discussed here can help in the development and specification of a general approach—one that is broadly protective of falsehoods, including lies, but that carves out important exceptions. The focus is on the role of government, but I shall have something to say about the obligations of private institutions as well.

ACTUAL MALICE AND BEYOND

In the modern era, a pervasive concern is the dissemination of falsehoods about actual or potential public officials.[2] The falsehoods might be innocent, negligent, or intentional. They might not expose people to ridicule or contempt, or count as defamatory, but they might be false, embarrassing, disruptive, or damaging even so.

Importantly, they might be *positive*, as, for example, in a statement that a particular candidate served with great distinction in the military, competed in the Olympics, performed specified heroic actions, or invented some technology. People exaggerate on their resumés; they lie. Certain forms of lying are unlawful in connection with applications for federal employment. Could it be made a crime to lie in any application for a job? Could it be made a crime to lie on a resumé? With respect to political campaigns, we could easily imagine a broader legislative effort to protect the truth. A law might say, for example, that speakers may be fined for knowingly spreading lies about candidates for public office; it might go further and target recklessness or negligence as well.[3] Analogues can be found in existing law, and they have sometimes been upheld.[4]

It is essential here to focus on the question of harm. Consistent with the framework sketched in Chapter 2, innocuous falsehoods should never be suppressed. If someone says that he is a little taller than he actually is, or that he weighs a bit less, there is no sufficient justification for punishing him. If a candidate for public office overstates his enthusiasm for the local sports team—if he says he is a lifelong fan, and if that is a lie—well, that's politics. A serious effort to excise lies from life, political or otherwise, would be a kind of nightmare, the stuff of science fiction or perhaps horror. Let us simply stipulate that life is full of falsehoods and many lies do not cause enough harm to justify any kind of legal intervention. In such cases, societies often can rely on good norms, which deter the worst kinds of lies (say, between co-workers, friends, or spouses). In terms of the legal system, we really need significant harm.

If libel itself is involved, of course, *New York Times* and later cases set out the governing standards. But suppose no libel is involved, perhaps because the technical requirements are not quite met, or perhaps because the falsehood casts a person in an appealing light, or perhaps because the relevant statement does not involve a person at all. In addition to the examples above, it might be said, for example, that a presidential candidate opposed the Affordable Care

Act when she strongly supported it; that she wanted to repeal the Second Amendment when she did not; that she spent six months studying Karl Marx in Moscow when she never visited Moscow at all; that she wanted to ban hunting when she did not; that she had a torrid romance with a famous movie star when she did nothing of the kind; that she never went to law school when she graduated with honors. Let us simply stipulate that none of these statements is libelous. Or suppose that someone lies or spreads falsehoods about public health and safety—about COVID-19, about cigarettes, about antibiotics, about chemicals. If and because there is harm, should public officials be able to respond? How?

"ZERO PEOPLE IN THE UNITED STATES OF AMERICA HAVE DIED FROM THE CORONAVIRUS"

For a glimpse of the sheer power of public statements, consider a careful study, finding that such statements on television significantly increased the spread of COVID-19—and spiked the number of deaths.[5] The team of researchers, led by the University of Chicago's Leonardo Bursztyn, studied the effects of the two most widely watched cable news shows in the United States: *Hannity* and *Tucker Carlson Tonight.* Both shows are on Fox News, which is relevant not only because of its large number of viewers but also because they are disproportionately elderly (and so more vulnerable to death or serious complications from COVID-19). As it turned out, Carlson and Hannity took very different approaches to COVID-19.

From late January, Tucker Carlson was genuinely concerned and signaled that the risks were serious:

> All of a sudden the Chinese coronavirus is looking like a real
> threat, that could be a global epidemic or even a pandemic. It's

impossible to know. But, it's the kind of thing that could be very serious—very serious.

Carlson continued to speak in this way in early February. By contrast, Sean Hannity was dismissive well into March. On February 27, he said this:

> And today, thankfully, zero people in the United States of America have died from the coronavirus. Zero. Now, let's put this in perspective. In 2017, 61,000 people in this country died from influenza, the flu. Common flu. Around 100 people die every single day from car wrecks.

On March 10, Hannity spoke in a similar vein:

> So far in the United States, there has been around 30 deaths, most of which came from one nursing home in the state of Washington. Healthy people, generally, 99 percent recover very fast, even if they contract it.

It was not until mid-March that Hannity changed his tune and began to treat the problem as a serious one.

To test the impact of these disparate approaches, Bursztyn and his collaborators surveyed 1,045 Fox News viewers of the age of fifty-five or older, asking about whether they changed their behavior in response to the pandemic—for example, by canceling travel plans, washing their hands more often, or engaging in social distancing. The researchers also asked people which shows they watched and the frequency with which they watched them, making it possible to test whether they were more likely to watch Carlson or Hannity.

The surveys found that Carlson's warnings mattered. Compared to other viewers of Fox News, his viewers changed their behavior relatively early. Hannity's lack of concern in February also mattered. Compared to other viewers of Fox News, his viewers changed their behavior relatively late.

Bursztyn and his collaborators also explored whether Carlson and Hannity affected the number of infections and deaths. The empirical questions here are challenging to answer. The researchers did some complicated detective work, with plenty of moving parts. These included data on COVID-19 cases and deaths at the county level, measured by day, and also Nielsen's viewership data for both shows, again looking at day-by-day figures.

The basic finding is simple: In places where more people were watching Hannity than Carlson, there were significantly more COVID-19 cases and death. In short, greater exposure to Hannity relative to Carlson "increased the number of total cases and deaths." Importantly, the differences between Hannity viewers and Carlson viewers started to fall in mid-March. That is consistent with the fact that the two hosts began to converge in their coverage right around that time.

This is only one study, of course, and I am not suggesting that in a system committed to freedom of speech, anything said by Hannity should be regulable in any way. The importance of the study is that it provides evidence of the potentially harmful effects of what trusted people say on television. Such accounts can much affect behavior. The magnitude of the effects will depend on how much people trust the source and on how much information people think they have in advance. If a television host says that dropped objects do not fall or that cats can talk, viewers are unlikely to believe them. But if a television host falsely says that a politician has committed a crime, and if that host is generally taken to be credible, the false statement might be widely believed. The same is certainly true with respect to information that bears on public health, at least when viewers do not start with a strong conviction to the contrary.

TENSION

I have suggested that government should be allowed to regulate falsehoods that threaten to cause serious harm that cannot be avoided through a more speech-protective route. I have also suggested that insofar as we are dealing with lies, the government's burden is lowered. How do these proposals fit with current law? What guidance do they give? Insofar as we are speaking of political speech and campaigns, they support a strong presumption: the government should keep its hands off, even when falsehoods and lies are involved.

Under *New York Times*, we might think that the right question is whether there is actual malice. Though *New York Times* applied the actual malice standard to libel, it might be expanded to cover many other false statements: If the speaker knew that his statements were false or acted with reckless indifference to the question of truth or falsity, the Constitution might permit the government to impose punishment, regulation, or liability. If *New York Times* can be extended in that way, then regulation of many false political statements would stand on firm ground. Indeed, falsehoods on a resumé would be punishable, certainly if the writer knows that the statements are false (as is typically the case). On the other hand, *Alvarez* seems to make it clear that the free speech principle does not allow the law to go nearly so far. Consistent with the approach defended here, the case seems to hold that even intentional falsehoods are generally protected unless they cause serious harm that cannot be avoided through speech-protective alternatives.

The plurality also in *Alvarez* gave great weight to whether the speech in question falls into time-honored categories of cases in which the government has forbidden false statements. Implicitly drawing on the thought of Edmund Burke, the plurality seems to have thought that if a conclusion is time-honored, it deserves respect. The plurality was reluctant to add new categories of regulable falsehoods, apparently on the theory that longevity creates a kind of legitimacy. Because it goes beyond libel, broad regulation of lies and falsehoods in political campaigns cannot claim longevity. But the basic point is that under *Alvarez*, intentional falsehoods enjoy a great deal of protection to the extent that they can be countered with more speech, rather than enforced silence.

For that reason, *New York Times* and *Alvarez* are in evident and serious tension: Under the reasoning of *Alvarez*, *New York Times* would seem to have done far too little to protect speech. After all, counterspeech might be used to respond to a libelous statement, even if the actual malice standard is met. Shouldn't the *New York Times* Court have recognized that point, at least if *Alvarez* is correct? If we agree with the holding and reasoning in *Alvarez*, shouldn't we conclude that if someone knowingly lies about someone, and defames that person, the remedy is counterspeech? If someone says that a presidential candidate committed a violent crime and knows that the statement is false, counterspeech—and not a damage action—might be the constitutionally required response. And indeed, that does seem to be the logic of *Alvarez*, which emphasizes that in the face of an intentional falsehood about receipt of the Congressional Medal of Honor, the constitutionally mandated remedy is counterspeech. And yet *Alvarez* does not question *New York Times*.

One way to square the two decisions is to return to the *Alvarez* plurality opinion and emphasize history, not abstract theory. The idea of libel is time-honored; it has been around for a very long time. That means that the Court will allow libel actions, so long as they are suitably constrained. By contrast, history does not contain a general exception for false statements of fact, even if they count as lies. Apart from history, we might think that libelous statements are indeed difficult to meet with counterspeech, and that the harm is so immediate and so likely, and often so serious, that a damage remedy is legitimate. With a false claim about having received the Congressional Medal of Honor, we have a form of pathetically narcissistic lying. But it can be corrected, and in terms of harm, it is not nearly as grave as libel. If someone falsely says that a governor or a musician has raped someone, we are dealing with a much more serious matter.

Where does this leave regulation of falsehoods in a political campaign? If such regulation goes beyond libel, there is a strong argument that it is constitutionally invalid under the principle I have defended and under *Alvarez*, except insofar as it reaches statements that cause serious harm and that cannot be sufficiently reduced through counterspeech. The meaning of that exception, signaled by *Alvarez* and endorsed here, is less than entirely clear. Courts would undoubtedly be tempted to conclude that politics is a mean business and that most of the time, counterspeech is the right remedy. But if someone intentionally spreads a falsehood, and if the falsehood has an adverse effect on the democratic process, is it really right to insist that the Constitution forbids the government from imposing some kind of sanction or remedy? Is that so clear?

It is probably clear enough. We have good reason to fear the potential bias of any enforcing entity, particularly if it is in the hands of a political actor (such as a president or prime minister) with clear political incentives. For that reason, there is a strong argument in favor of treading cautiously if at all. If there is to be a response, the best one might be mandatory warnings or disclosure; that response might be used online. There is also a strong argument in favor of ensuring that any regulation of falsehoods in politics is enforced by an independent agency, such as or akin to the Federal Election Commission. The proposals sketched above—including a modest monetary penalty and a right to some kind of retraction—might well be adapted to accommodate the relevant interests.

Of course, television stations, newspapers, and social media providers have much more room to maneuver. Unconstrained by the First Amendment, they can respond to dirty tricks as they see fit. In view of the evident risks posed by false statements about political candidates, Facebook, Twitter, and YouTube might do more than they are now doing to regulate or take down such statements, even if they are made in political advertisements. It is not enough to say that counterspeech is the right remedy. To be sure, it is reasonable to distrust social media providers. Who appointed them to be the truth police? Why should they assume that role? I will turn to these issues shortly.

DEEPFAKES AND DOCTORED VIDEOS

Libel is an old issue, but something like libel, and sometimes a modern version of the thing itself, comes from deepfakes: products of techniques, based on artificial intelligence or machine learning, for creating apparently real images or videos, in which people might be shown doing or saying something that they never did or said.[6] If an image of a person can be found, the technology is now available to make it look as if that person despises his country, engages in shoplifting, or dances wildly to Rolling Stones songs—anything at all. Deepfake pornography is now pervasive.[7] Deepfakes could easily be used to discredit candidates for public office.

Let us understand "doctored videos" as products of techniques by which a real video is altered to make it seem as if people are doing or saying something other than what they did, or differently from how they did it.[8] A doctored video might show people supporting a cause that they abhor, committing a crime, showing disloyalty to their country, acting inappropriately when they did nothing of the kind, or being inebriated or otherwise impaired. In some cases, doctored videos are quite credible, in the sense that viewers do not believe that they have been doctored. They might turn out to be libelous.[9] I will be mostly speaking here of deepfakes, but the analysis applies to doctored videos as well.

For orientation—and for a sense of what is coming—consider some hypothetical cases:

- Jane Jones is a high school teacher. A deepfake shows her in a romantic situation with a student.
- Philip Cross is a candidate for public office. A deepfake shows him endorsing Hitler and the Holocaust.
- John Simons is eighty years old. A deepfake shows him taking an "energy pill" and then competing fiercely and well in a pickup basketball game.
- A deepfake shows the Beatles playing Taylor Swift songs.
- A deepfake shows the Mona Lisa speaking like a teenager.
- A deepfake shows a Labrador retriever dancing like Michael Jackson.
- A deepfake shows the attorney general of the United States looking drunk and disoriented.

Alvarez might well be taken to suggest that deepfakes cannot be regulated simply because they are deepfakes. They are essentially falsehoods, and to that extent, they are protected unless they cause harm.[10] Do they cause any? For people who are used in deepfakes, harm takes the form of reputational injury. A deepfake can be favorable or innocuous, but it can also be akin to or a form of defamation; it can hold people up to ridicule or contempt in their communities. If it is defamatory—if its propositional content amounts to a libel—it can be regulated under the standards of *New York Times* and *Gertz*. Apart from injuring the person who is depicted, it can injure the community by, for example, discrediting a candidate for public office and thus distorting the democratic process.

But deepfakes, as such, need not be libelous at all. They might be positive; they might make people look impressive or wonderful. For example, they might show a member of Congress playing tennis or golf at a professional level. And if people do not believe that a deepfake is real, there should be no harm. If a rock group from the 1960s (two members of whom are dead) is seen playing songs by a contemporary musician, we are dealing with something like whimsy, humor, or satire—all of which should be protected by the First Amendment.[11] The risk of harm arises if and when people think that what they are seeing actually happened. If people are falsely shown in a romantic situation or endorsing a political position that they abhor, they may in fact be harmed. In this light, consider the following proposition: *The government can regulate or ban deepfakes, consistent with the First Amendment, if (1) it is not reasonably obvious or explicitly and prominently disclosed that they are deepfakes, and (2) they would create serious reputational harm.* Note that (2) is meant to build on but go beyond the existing law of libel.[12]

Here is a possible response, inspired by the prevailing opinion in *Alvarez*: The best response to a deepfake is counterspeech and disclosure, not censorship. That is true for both private institutions and public officials. The idea of "reputational harm" is too vague. A social media provider might conclude that platform users should be notified that deepfakes are deepfakes; it might reject the view that doctored videos should be taken down. It might conclude that users should be able to see those videos so long as they receive the information they need to put the videos into perspective. As the plurality put it in *Alvarez*: "The remedy for speech that is false is speech that is true. This is the ordinary course in a free society."[13] Twitter has adopted an approach of this kind, requiring labels for manipulated media (and also taking down tweets if they are "likely to cause harm").[14]

As a matter of constitutional law, something similar might be said about what governments may do. Perhaps they should be required to choose the approach that is maximally protective of speech. In *Alvarez*, for example, the plurality explained: "The Government has not shown, and cannot show, why counterspeech would not suffice to achieve its interest. The facts of this case indicate that the dynamics of free speech, of counterspeech, of refutation, can overcome the lie."[15] It added: "There is, however, at least one less speech-restrictive means by which the Government could likely protect the integrity of the military awards system. A Government-created database could list Congressional Medal of Honor winners. Were a database accessible through the Internet, it would be easy to verify and expose false claims."[16]

But it would be difficult to defend the view that this is a sufficient response to deepfakes. If someone is portrayed as doing something that she never did or as endorsing a position that she despises, an accessible database would be most unlikely to undo the damage. Perhaps the speech-protective approach would be clear disclosure, informing people, before they see the video, that it is fake. Under *Alvarez*, there should be no constitutional barrier to that kind of control on deepfakes, at least on a sufficient showing of harm—and the same analysis applies to doctored videos.[17] What is that sufficient showing? Libel is a good answer, but it is not the only one. If people get the impression that someone did something that they did not do, there can be harm for that very reason.

Should government be permitted to go beyond disclosure? More aggressive controls might take the form of fines and an order to cease and desist, enforced perhaps by an independent commission. Or they could operate via a tort-like approach, operating through a civil cause of action, building on libel law, and creating a kind of property right in one's person.

It is tempting to respond that, in an important sense, deepfakes and doctored videos are nothing new. They are equivalent to false statements of fact. If a deepfake depicts the attorney general looking drunk and disoriented, perhaps it is not so different, or any different, from this apparently credible statement: "I saw the Attorney General looking drunk and disoriented." The propositional content of deepfakes, in the form of such statements, is not regulated or banned (unless there is an independent ground—for example, they might be defamatory or obscene). Why should deepfakes themselves be treated differently?

A reasonable answer is that deepfakes (and doctored videos) have a unique kind of authenticity; they are more credible than merely verbal representations. In a sense, they are self-authenticating. The human mind does not easily dismiss them, and if it does, there is some part of it that remains convinced. Recall that behavioral science makes a distinction between two families of cognitive operations in the human mind: System 1, which is fast and automatic, and System 2, which is more deliberative and slower.[18] System 1 and System 2 do not distinguish between deepfakes and reality. Once System 2 is properly informed, System 1 is likely to remain under the influence; it hears a kind of mental echo. (Recall the discussion of truth bias.) If you see a deepfake of a drunk attorney general, you will have a hard time getting the image out of your mind. For these reasons, it is plausible to say that deepfakes (and doctored videos) are properly the objects of regulatory attention even if statements that embody their propositional content are not. And as we have seen, some false statements of fact, seriously harmful to the political process, may be regulable even if they are not defamatory.

For private institutions, an aggressive approach would be quite reasonable (more on that below). For government, a prominent disclosure mandate should be upheld for deepfakes and doctored videos. On the logic of *Alvarez*, a ban or fine would be difficult to defend. Under the constitutional test I have proposed, it is a genuinely difficult question whether bans or fines on deepfakes should be upheld. If they are libelous, of course, the usual standards apply. If they are not libelous, I think that bans or mandates should be struck down in light of the availability of clear, prominent disclosure requirements.

WHAT FACEBOOK DID

These conclusions have strong implications for television networks and for social media platforms such as Facebook, YouTube, and Twitter. Imaginable restrictions could protect, separately or at once, democratic processes and individual lives. In 2019, Facebook responded to considerations of this general kind with an announcement that it is banning deepfakes.[19] That is an important step in the right direction. But is it enough?

As Facebook pointed out in its thoughtful announcement, media can be manipulated for benign reasons, such as making video sharper and audio clearer. Some forms of manipulation are clearly meant as jokes, satires, parodies, or political statements—as, for example, when a rock star or a politician is depicted as a giant or as having superpowers. That is not a basis for regulation by government or by Facebook. Under its policy, Facebook says that it will remove "misleading manipulative media" only if two conditions are met:

- "It has been edited or synthesized—beyond adjustments for clarity or quality—in ways that aren't apparent to an average person and would likely mislead someone into thinking that a subject of the video said words that they did not actually say."

- "It is the product of artificial intelligence or machine learning that merges, replaces or superimposes content onto a video, making it appear to be authentic."

In a sense, the first condition is close to what I have suggested here. The average person must, by hypothesis, be reasonable. There is no requirement of serious harm (and perhaps there should be no such requirement insofar as we are dealing with regulation by a private institution, not a government). The two conditions are meant to be tailored to Facebook's concern: use of new or emerging technologies to mislead the average person into thinking that someone said something that they never said.

Facebook's announcement also makes it clear that even if a video is not removed under the new policy, other safeguards might be triggered.[20] If, for example, a video contains graphic violence or nudity, it will be taken down.

Facebook's current approach should be seen as significant progress over what preceded it, and other social media platforms would do well to consider it. YouTube's approach is both more and less aggressive; it flatly forbids "video content that has been technically manipulated (beyond clips taken out of context) to fabricate events where there is a serious risk of egregious harm."[21] Note that YouTube imposes a requirement of egregious harm, as Facebook does not. The term is lamentably vague, but it is clearly meant to allow manipulated media that is funny or satirical, or that is meant as some kind of commentary.

For Facebook's approach, two problems remain. The first is that even if a deepfake is involved, the policy does not apply if the deepfake depicts deeds rather than words. (Recall the first condition, suggesting that the deepfake must depict a subject of the video saying "words that they did not actually say.") Suppose that artificial intelligence is used to show a political candidate working with terrorists, beating up a small child, or using heroin. Nothing in the new policy would address those depictions. That is a serious gap. Deepfakes should be banned on Facebook and other platforms if they present actions that would otherwise fall within the prohibition, even if no one is shown to have said anything.

The second problem is that the prohibition is limited to products of artificial intelligence or machine learning. But why? Suppose that videos are altered in other ways—for example, by slowing them down so as to make someone appear drunk or drugged, as in the case of an infamous doctored video of Nancy Pelosi. Or suppose that a series of videos, directed against a candidate for governor, are produced not with artificial intelligence or machine learning, but nonetheless in such a way as to run afoul of the first condition; that is, they have been edited or synthesized so as to make the average person think that the candidate said words that she did not actually say. What matters is not the particular technology used to deceive people, but whether unacceptable deception has occurred.

FALSEHOODS ON SOCIAL MEDIA

The considerations raised here suggest that Facebook, Twitter, and YouTube have done some excellent work in controlling misinformation. At the same time, they raise serious doubts about Facebook's policy in favor of allowing falsehoods in campaign advertisements. By exempting "politicians" from its third-party fact-checking program, designed to reduce the spread of lies and falsehoods in ads, the company is essentially throwing up its hands. With some urgency, it should be seeking new ways to reduce the risk that lies and falsehoods will undermine the democratic process.

To its credit, Facebook takes a number of steps to reduce the spread of falsehoods. If information has been independently debunked by its third-party fact-checkers, the company will reduce its spread on News Feed.[22] In addition, "content across Facebook and Instagram that has been rated false or partly false by a third-party fact-checker" is "prominently labeled so that people can better decide for themselves what to read, trust and share."[23] The labels are shown on top of false and partly false photos and videos, and they link to the assessment from the fact-checker. This is part of the company's goal of "empowering people to decide for themselves what to read, trust, and share by informing them with more context and promoting news literacy."

With respect to some advertisements, Facebook goes further. It flatly "prohibits ads that include claims debunked by third-party fact checkers or, in certain circumstances, claims debunked by organizations with particular expertise."[24] The policy extends to "misinformation about vaccines as identified and verified by global health organizations such as the World Health Organization." Note too that before the 2018 midterms, Facebook expanded its voter suppression policies to include certain misrepresentations (i.e., when to vote, where to vote, voter qualifications) and threats of violence. Under its policy, all such posts are to be removed from the platform once detected (usually by the Facebook system itself, but also through reports). With respect to elections, Twitter has related policies,[25] as does YouTube, which bans "deliberately telling voters an incorrect election date" and "giving made up voter eligibility requirements," as by saying that voting is available only to people who are over fifty years old.[26] And with respect to misinformation, Twitter uses labels and warnings, designed to reduce its influence and spread.[27]

Nick Clegg, Facebook's vice-president of global affairs and communications, has defended the company's exemption for political advertisements, arguing that they belong in an altogether different category and should not be reviewed for veracity. If a candidate for public office falsely says that his opponent served time for attempted murder, is a drug addict, participated in terrorist activities, or tried to bribe foreign officials—apparently Facebook will do nothing. Clegg explains: "We are champions of free speech and defend it in the face of attempts to restrict it. Censoring or stifling political discourse would be at odds with what we are about."

At the same time, he announced one exception to the exemption for politicians: "previously debunked content." If a politician shares content that has been debunked by fact-checkers in the past, that content will not be allowed in advertisements. But if it is a new falsehood, it will be allowed. In short, Facebook does "not submit speech by politicians to our independent fact-checkers, and we generally allow it on the platform even when it would otherwise breach our normal content rules." But why, exactly? Any broadcaster, and any social-media platform, is legally entitled to refuse to run ads that contain palpable lies.

Drawing on Mill, the best argument on Facebook's behalf would point to the exceptional difficulty of policing truth or falsity. It can be hard to distinguish between fact ("my opponent committed a crime") and opinion ("my opponent belongs in jail"). In some cases, factual errors will be both clear and demonstrable. Taken in isolation, they should not be allowed. But if Facebook got in the business of taking down clear and demonstrable errors in political ads, you can see why it might soon find itself regretting it. Politicians of all kinds would soon accuse their opponents of lying about them—and ask Facebook to remove their ads. The company's decisions would predictably be subject to claims of political bias.

Whether those charges were opportunistic or sincere, Facebook might well conclude that it makes more sense to adopt a general rule: allow a free-for-all. Fair enough. But we have seen that with the help of social-media platforms, lies and misinformation are instantly spreading to countless people. With algorithms and personalization, those who spread falsehoods are increasingly able to reach receptive audiences and tailor their messages to them. The problem is only going to get worse.

That threatens to create a political order in which ordinary citizens cannot know what is true, and in which they end up believing those who are best at fooling them, or who have the most power. (From George Orwell's *1984*: "The party told you to reject the evidence of your eyes and ears. It was their final, most essential command.") To address that danger, it is not enough to rely on abstractions about the importance of freedom of speech. Even for political advertisements, social media platforms might, for example, consider enlisting the law of defamation, and treat clearly defamatory statements, directed at one politician against another, as beyond the pale. For false statements of various kinds, they might use less intrusive tools, such as warnings and disclosure. Facebook in particular might build on its own practice in creating an independent oversight board, giving such a body a degree of authority to take down demonstrable falsehoods that promise to cause serious harm. Following the practice in some nations, it might refuse to air political advertisements in the period immediately preceding an election.

It is easy to understand Facebook's reluctance to operate any kind of Ministry of Truth. But *1984* is one thing; the present is another. Facebook and other social-media platforms have made significant strides in combating misinformation. But in some ways, they are contributing to a situation that diminishes the power of truth in democratic debate every day. That endangers democracy itself. The question remains: What are they, or we, going to do about it?

HEALTH AND SAFETY

We have seen that many falsehoods, including lies, involve health and safety. The first question is whether public officials have the authority to regulate them. The second question is what private institutions should do. Again, the first question implicates the Constitution; the second does not.

It is clear that insofar as we are dealing with false advertising, officials have a great deal of power. If someone falsely claims that a product would prevent heart disease or would not have adverse side effects, the government can impose a stiff fine. Thank goodness for that. Commercial advertising does not lie at the core of what the free speech principle is about, and an advertisement that threatens to endanger health or safety creates a sufficiently serious risk of harm.

Suppose, however, that we are not dealing with commercial advertising but instead with a scientific, medical, or other claim, perhaps made for reasons of self-interest, perhaps made as a result of a mistake, perhaps made for other reasons. The easiest cases for regulation are at the intersection of *New York Times v. Sullivan*[28] and *Brandenburg v. Ohio*:[29] (1) the speakers know that what they are saying is false (and so there is actual malice) and (2) the claim creates a clear and present danger of harm. In such cases, the argument for allowing regulation seems clear-cut. It is almost as clear-cut if we slightly weaken (1) and if the speakers do not actually know that what they are saying is false, but are recklessly indifferent to the question of truth or falsity. In such cases, the actual malice standard is also met.

Some of the weakest cases for regulation are those in which (1) the speakers are negligent but sincerely believe that what they are saying is true and (2) the claim creates a danger, but it is hard to say that it is imminent, and while it will probably come to fruition, it can be avoided by counterspeech, at least in principle. Something like this is true of a wide variety of people who cast doubt on claims about health risks—involving COVID-19, smoking, obesity, infrequent exercise, excessive consumption of salt and sugar. Even if we stipulate that those claims are false, a system of freedom of expression does best if it does not regulate cases involving (1) and (2). The arguments for protecting falsehoods, elaborated in Chapter 5, strongly argue against imposing restrictions in such cases.

In this light, we should be able to identify the intermediate cases. In some of them, (1) the speakers do not believe that what they are saying is true and (2) the claim creates a danger, but it is hard to say that it is imminent, and while it will probably come to fruition, it can be avoided by counterspeech, at least in principle. In my view, regulation is legitimate in such cases. The speakers are lying, and lying does not deserve as much protection as unintentional false-hood. The presence of a real danger is enough to justify regulation of lies. We are dealing with something like fraud.

In other cases, (1) the speakers believe that what they are saying is true, but it is actually false and (2) the claim creates a clear and present danger of harm. Such cases are harder for regulators, because speakers are acting in good faith. But if what they are saying is false, and if the harm is both imminent and likely, regulation should not be ruled out-of-bounds by the free speech principle. Of course it is true that in such cases, it is essential to ensure that independent tribunals are available to assess the relevant questions—and that public officials meet a high burden of proof.

What about social media companies? Facebook has a policy in favor of taking down "misinformation that contributes to the risk of imminent violence or physical harm." It is important to emphasize that the test has three prongs: (1) the information must be false *and* (2) the risk to which it contributes must be of *imminent* (3) violence or physical harm. The formulation is close to the clear and present danger test, especially insofar as the emphasis is on a risk of "imminent" violence or physical harm. In the context of COVID-19, Facebook would take down false statements that suggest that if you ingest certain products, you will be cured or rendered immune, or that you are not at risk if you are under fifty years old. Similarly,

Facebook has made it clear that if people say "social distancing does not work" or "wearing a mask makes you sick," their post will be taken down. The test does not specify what level of probability is high enough to create a "risk."

But if the risk is not of *imminent* violence or harm, the misinformation is allowed (though it is subject to various policies calling for the use of labeling and other tools applied to factual claims found to be false by third-party fact-checkers).[30] Suppose, for example, that someone posted, "cigarettes do not cause cancer, heart disease, or any other harm," or "seatbelt buckling increases your risks of death," or "sugar and salt are great for your health—the more the better!" Because the risk of harm is not imminent, these falsehoods would not be taken down. As Facebook leadership has explained, "There's something about speech where the risk is immediate, where there is not necessarily going to be time for debate, that makes that speech especially important for us to address."[31]

Facebook deserves credit for taking significant steps to protect against violence or physical harm, and other companies would do well to build on this standard. But there is a reasonable argument that the imminence requirement is too strict. In cases in which we are dealing with a genuine lie and a serious risk of violence or harm in (say) two weeks or even two years, should the statement be allowed? That is not at all clear.[32] Actually let's put it more strongly. The answer is: No.

THE FRAMEWORK REVISITED

Recall the relevance of four moving parts: the speakers' State of Mind (and hence their level of culpability); the Magnitude of Harm; the Likelihood of the Harm; and the Timing of Harm. As a reminder: With respect to State of Mind, people might be (1) lying,

(2) reckless, (3) negligent, and (4) reasonable but mistaken. With respect to Magnitude of Harm, we can distinguish among (1) grave, (2) moderate, (3) minor, and (4) nonexistent. With respect to Likelihood of Harm, we might have (1) inevitable, (2) more likely than not, (3) low probability, and (4) very low probability. For Timing of Harm, it might be (1) imminent, in the sense of immediate, (2) imminent, in the sense of the near future, (3) reasonably soon, or (4) not in the long term, but not reasonably soon.

We can understand *New York Times v. Sullivan* to say that unless there is (1) or (2) for State of Mind, constitutional protection is guaranteed, whatever the harm. *Alvarez* holds that even with (1) for State of Mind, constitutional protection is granted, if we have (3) or (4) for Likelihood of Harm (and perhaps for Magnitude of Harm as well). We can understand Facebook to say that material will be taken down with a (1), (2), (3), or (4) for State of Mind and a (1) or (2) for Timing of Harm (and perhaps a (1) or (2) for Magnitude of Harm).

I have questioned all of these conclusions, though for different reasons. Consider the case of defamation of public officials. In my view, the law may respond if we have a (3) or (4) for State of Mind, if and because we have a (1) or (2) for Magnitude of Harm. At the same time, I have suggested that the response must take modest forms. In *Alvarez*, I have suggested that we actually have (2) for Likelihood of Harm, and because we have (1) for State of Mind, constitutional protection should be denied. For Facebook generally, I have suggested that when we have (1) for State of Mind and (1) or (2) for Magnitude of Harm, material should be taken down even if we have (3) and perhaps even (4) for Timing of Harm.

By definition, producers of deepfakes and altered videos fall within (1) for State of Mind. In terms of Magnitude of Harm, Likelihood of Harm, and Imminence of Harm, we need to know some details. When all three seem to be at least (2), there is a sufficient justification for regulation, whether we are speaking of public officials or social media providers. Speaking very generally, and with the goal of helping to orient concrete cases, I urge that if we have (1) for State of Mind, and at least (2) for Magnitude of Harm, the free speech principle ought not to stand in the way of government regulation. It would also be reasonable to say that if we have (3) or (4) for State of Mind, there should be a strong presumption in favor of allowing freedom of speech, to be overcome, perhaps, only when we have a clear (1) for Magnitude of Harm.

CHAPTER NINE

Truth Matters

IN LIFE AND in politics, truth matters. In the end, it might matter more than anything else. It is a precondition for trust and hence for cooperation. But what, exactly, can governments do to restrict the dissemination of falsehoods in systems committed to freedom of speech? In brief: Much less than some of them want, but much more than some of them are now doing.

I have argued in favor of a general principle: *False statements are constitutionally protected unless the government can show that they threaten to cause serious harm that cannot be avoided through a more speech-protective route.* I have also suggested that when lies are involved, the government may impose regulation on the basis of a weaker demonstration of harm than is ordinarily required for unintentional falsehoods. Reasonable people can disagree about how to apply these ideas in concrete cases. In general, however, this general principle, and the accompanying suggestion, give a great deal of constitutional protection to falsehoods and even lies.

In the United States, the Supreme Court has often said that false statements are valueless and that the First Amendment does not protect them. At the same time, the Court has long held that the First Amendment imposes serious restrictions on defamation actions and that many false statements are indeed protected by that amendment. In *Alvarez*, the Court ruled that false statements are protected unless the government can produce a powerful justification for regulating or banning them. The Court has explained this conclusion largely by pointing to the risk that regulating falsehoods might deter truth.

The specific conclusion in *Alvarez* is difficult to defend. Is it really important to protect someone's demonstrably false claim that he won the Congressional Medal of Honor? The answer is no. But in many cases, the argument for protecting false statements of fact is much stronger: a denial that climate change is real, an erroneous report on a prominent politician, an exaggerated statement about the risks posed by genetically modified organisms. There are strong reasons to protect falsehoods. The government's own judgments about what is true and what is false might not be trustworthy. Regulation of false statements might and probably will chill truthful statements. People can learn from false statements; our engagement with falsity can deepen our understanding. It is important for people to know what other people think, even if what they think is not true. Banning false statements can simply drive them underground and increase their power and allure; counterspeech can be far better and even more effective than prohibition.

The problem is that taken individually or as a whole, these arguments do not support the broad conclusion that a system of free expression must always give strong protection to falsehoods and lies. Some falsehoods, and some lies, make broad propositions of this kind seem inadequate or even silly. Some of these involve time-honored prohibitions: consider perjury, fraud, and false commercial advertising. Some of them involve current or coming problems;

considered doctored videos and deepfakes. A central point is that governments have a large and growing toolbox. Especially because so much speech occurs online, they might consider creative tools for reducing the spread of falsehoods, such as disclosures, labels, warnings, disclaimers, and uses of choice architecture.

These points offer a distinctive perspective on both old and new problems. They strongly suggest that in the United States, current constitutional law fails to strike the right balance. Public officials, actors, musicians, and athletes should be able to do far more than they are now permitted to do to respond to defamation. The same is true for ordinary citizens subject to damaging falsehoods. In addition, public officials have considerable power to regulate deepfakes and doctored videos. They are also entitled to act to protect public health and safety, certainly in the context of lies, and if falsehoods create sufficiently serious risks, to control such falsehoods as well. In all of these contexts, some of the most promising tools do not involve censorship or punishment; they involve more speech-protective approaches, such as labels and warnings.

Private institutions, including television networks, magazines, newspapers, and social media providers, should be acting more aggressively to control defamation and other falsehoods and lies. They should be doing more than they are now doing to prevent the spread of misinformation involving health and safety and of doctored videos. They should reduce the coming spread of deepfakes.

These are specific conclusions, but they bear on some of the largest and most general questions in all of politics and law, and indeed in daily life itself. Hannah Arendt put it this way: "What is at stake here is this common and factual reality itself, and this is indeed a political problem of the first order."[1] The principle of freedom of speech should not be taken to forbid efforts to protect reality.

Appendix

...

This appendix reprints relevant standards of Facebook, Twitter, and YouTube as of June 2020. It is important to emphasize that by the companies' own account, these are works in progress, subject to improvement with new circumstances and understandings. Nonetheless, they provide an illuminating glimpse of the state of the art, and also of current challenges. As emphasized in the main text, they also bear on constitutional issues. Courts often ask government to consider the most speech-protective alternatives, and the private sector has been inventive in identifying approaches that combat misinformation while maintaining a commitment to freedom of speech. As also discussed in the main text, I do not believe that the existing standards always strike the right balance.

FACEBOOK—COMMUNITY STANDARDS

Violence and Incitement

Policy Rationale

We aim to prevent potential offline harm that may be related to content on Facebook. While we understand that people commonly express disdain or disagreement by threatening or calling for violence in non-serious ways, we remove language that incites or facilitates serious violence. We remove content, disable accounts, and work with law enforcement when we believe there is a genuine risk of physical harm or direct threats to public safety. We also try to consider the language and context in order to distinguish casual statements from content that constitutes a credible threat to public or personal safety. In determining whether a threat is credible, we may also consider additional information like a person's public visibility and the risks to their physical safety.

Do Not Post

– Imagery of private individuals or minor public figures that has been manipulated to include threats of violence either in text or pictorial (adding bulls eye, dart, gun to head, etc.).
– Misinformation and unverifiable rumors that contribute to the risk of imminent violence or physical harm.

Misinformation

Policy: Facebook prohibits ads that include claims debunked by third-party fact checkers or, in certain circumstances, claims debunked by organizations with particular expertise. Advertisers that repeatedly post information deemed to be false may have restrictions placed on their ability to advertise on Facebook. . . .

Examples:

– Ads containing claims which are debunked by third-party fact-checkers

– Ads which include misinformation about vaccines as identified and verified by global health organizations such as the World Health Organization

Misrepresentation

Policy Rationale: Authenticity is the cornerstone of our community. We believe that people are more accountable for their statements and actions when they use their authentic identities. That's why we require people to connect on Facebook using the name they go by in everyday life. Our authenticity policies are intended to create a safe environment where people can trust and hold one another accountable.

Do not:

– Misrepresent your identity by
  • Using a name that does not abide by our name policies
  • Providing a false date of birth
– Misuse our products by
  • Creating a profile for someone under thirteen years old
  • Maintaining multiple accounts
  • Creating inauthentic profiles
  • Sharing an account with any other person
  • Creating another Facebook account after being banned from the site
  • Creating or Managing a Page, Group, Event or Instagram Profile because the previous Page, Group, Event or Instagram Profile was removed from the site
  • Evading the registration requirements outlined in our Terms of Service

- Impersonate others by
  - Using their images with the explicit aim to deceive people
  - Creating a profile assuming the persona of or speaking for another person or entity
  - Creating a Page assuming to be or speak for another person or entity for whom the user is not authorized to do so.
  - Posting imagery that is likely to deceive the public as to the content's origin, if:
    - The entity or an authorized representative objects to the content, and
    - Can establish a risk of harm to members of the public.

False News

Policy Rationale: Reducing the spread of false news on Facebook is a responsibility that we take seriously. We also recognize that this is a challenging and sensitive issue. We want to help people stay informed without stifling productive public discourse. There is also a fine line between false news and satire or opinion. For these reasons, we don't remove false news from Facebook but instead, significantly reduce its distribution by showing it lower in the News Feed. Learn more about our work to reduce the spread of false news here.

We are working to build a more informed community and reduce the spread of false news in a number of different ways, namely by

- Disrupting economic incentives for people, Pages, and domains that propagate misinformation
- Using various signals, including feedback from our community, to inform a machine learning model that predicts which stories may be false
- Reducing the distribution of content rated as false by independent third-party fact-checkers

- Empowering people to decide for themselves what to read, trust, and share by informing them with more context and promoting news literacy
- Collaborating with academics and other organizations to help solve this challenging issue

Manipulated Media

Policy Rationale

Media, including image, audio, or video, can be edited in a variety of ways. In many cases, these changes are benign, like a filter effect on a photo. In other cases, the manipulation isn't apparent and could mislead, particularly in the case of video content. We aim to remove this category of manipulated media when the criteria laid out below have been met.

In addition, we will continue to invest in partnerships (including with journalists, academics and independent fact-checkers) to help us reduce the distribution of false news and misinformation, as well as to better inform people about the content they encounter online.

Do not post:

Video

- that has been edited or synthesized, beyond adjustments for clarity or quality, in ways that are not apparent to an average person, and would likely mislead an average person to believe that a subject of the video said words that they did not say AND
- is the product of artificial intelligence or machine learning, including deep learning techniques (e.g., a technical deepfake), that merges, combines, replaces, and/or superimposes content onto a video, creating a video that appears authentic.

This policy does not extend to content that is parody or satire or is edited to omit words that were said or change the order of words that were said.

TWITTER PLATFORM MANIPULATION AND SPAM POLICY

You may not use Twitter's services in a manner intended to artificially amplify or suppress information or engage in behavior that manipulates or disrupts people's experience on Twitter.

. . .

Platform manipulation can take many forms and our rules are intended to address a wide range of prohibited behavior, including:

- commercially-motivated spam, that typically aims to drive traffic or attention from a conversation on Twitter to accounts, websites, products, services, or initiatives;
- inauthentic engagements, that attempt to make accounts or content appear more popular or active than they are; and
- coordinated activity, that attempts to artificially influence conversations through the use of multiple accounts, fake accounts, automation and/or scripting.

What is in violation of this policy? Under this policy we prohibit a range of behaviors in the following areas:

Accounts and identity:
You can't mislead others on Twitter by operating fake accounts. This includes using misleading account information to engage in spamming, abusive, or disruptive behavior. Some of the factors that we take into consideration include:

– use of stock or stolen profile photos, particularly those depicting other people;
– use of stolen or copied profile bios; and
– use of intentionally misleading profile information, including profile location.

You can't artificially amplify or disrupt conversations through the use of multiple accounts. This includes:

– <u>overlapping accounts</u>: operating multiple accounts with overlapping use cases, such as identical or similar personas or substantially similar content;
– <u>mutually interacting accounts:</u> operating multiple accounts that interact with one another in order to inflate or manipulate the prominence of specific Tweets or accounts; and
– <u>coordination:</u> creating multiple accounts to post duplicative content or create fake engagement, including:
  • posting identical or substantially similar Tweets or hashtags from multiple accounts you operate;
  • engaging (Retweets, Likes, mentions, Twitter Poll votes) repeatedly with the same Tweets or accounts from multiple accounts that you operate; and
  • coordinating with or compensating others to engage in artificial engagement or amplification, even if the people involved use only one account.

Engagement and metrics: You can't artificially inflate your own or others' followers or engagement. This includes:

– <u>selling/purchasing Tweet or account metric inflation:</u> selling or purchasing followers or engagements (Retweets, Likes, mentions, Twitter Poll votes);

- apps: using or promoting third-party services or apps that claim to add followers or add engagements to Tweets;
- reciprocal inflation: trading or coordinating to exchange follows or Tweet engagements (including but not limited to participation in "follow trains," "decks," and "Retweet for Retweet" behavior); and
- account transfers or sales: selling, purchasing, trading, or offering the sale, purchase, or trade of Twitter accounts, usernames, or temporary access to Twitter accounts.

. . .

What is not a violation of this policy? The following are not in violation of this policy:

- using Twitter pseudonymously or as a parody, commentary, or fan account;
- posting links without commentary occasionally; and
- operating multiple accounts with distinct identities, purposes, or use cases. These accounts may interact with one another, provided they don't violate other rules. Some examples include:
  • organizations with related but separate chapters or branches, such as a business with multiple locations;
  • operating a personal account in addition to pseudonymous accounts or accounts associated with your hobbies or initiatives; and
  • hobby/artistic bots.

YOUTUBE SPAM, DECEPTIVE PRACTICES & SCAMS POLICIES

YouTube doesn't allow spam, scams, or other deceptive practices that take advantage of the YouTube community. We also don't

allow content where the main purpose is to trick others into leaving
YouTube for another site. . . .

If you're posting content: Don't post content on YouTube if it fits any
of the descriptions noted below.

– <u>Video Spam</u>: Content that is excessively posted, repetitive, or
  untargeted and does one or more of the following:
  • Promises viewers they'll see something but instead directs
    them off site.
  • Gets clicks, views, or traffic off YouTube by promising viewers
    that they'll make money fast.
  • Sends audiences to sites that spread malware, try to gather
    personal information, or other sites that have a negative
    impact.
– <u>Misleading Metadata or Thumbnails</u>: Using the title, thumbnails,
  description, or tags to trick users into believing the content is
  something it is not.
– <u>Manipulated Media</u>: Content that has been technically manipulated or doctored in a way that misleads users (beyond clips taken
  out of context) and may pose a serious risk of egregious harm.
– <u>Scams</u>: Content offering cash gifts, "get rich quick" schemes, or
  pyramid schemes (sending money without a tangible product in a
  pyramid structure).
– <u>Voter Suppression</u>: Content aiming to mislead voters about the
  time, place, means or eligibility requirements for voting.
– <u>Suppression of Census Participation</u>: Content aiming to mislead
  participants about the time, means or eligibility requirements for
  participating in a census.

- Candidate Eligibility: Content that advances false claims related to the technical eligibility requirements for current political candidates and sitting elected government officials to serve in office. Eligibility requirements considered are based on applicable national law, and include age, citizenship, or vital status.
- Incentivization Spam: Content that sells engagement metrics such as views, likes, comments, or any other metric on YouTube. This also includes content where the only purpose is to boost subscribers, views, or other metrics (e.g. offering to subscribe to another creator's channel solely in exchange for them subscribing to your channel, also known as "Sub4Sub" content).
- Comments Spam: Comments where the sole purpose is to gather personal information from viewers, misleadingly drive viewers off YouTube, or perform any of the prohibited behaviors noted above.
- Repetitive comments: Leaving large amounts of identical, untargeted or repetitive comments.
- Live Stream Abuse: Live streams intended to stream content that belongs to somebody else and are not corrected following repeated warnings of possible abuse. Live streams should be actively monitored by the channel owner, and any potential issues should be corrected in a timely manner.

This policy applies to videos, video descriptions, comments, live streams, and any other YouTube product or feature. Keep in mind that this isn't a complete list.

   Note: You're allowed to encourage viewers to subscribe, hit the like button, share, or leave a comment.

Examples: Here are some examples of content that's not allowed on YouTube.

- Telling viewers they can vote through fake methods like texting their vote to a particular number
- Giving made up voter eligibility requirements like saying that a particular election is only open to voters over 50 years old
- Deliberately telling viewers an incorrect election date

More examples:

- Video Spam
- Misleading metadata or thumbnails
- Manipulated Media
- Voter Suppression and Suppression of Census Participation
- Candidate Eligibility
- Scams
- Incentivization Spam
- Comments Spam
- Live Stream Abuse

YOUTUBE COVID-19 MEDICAL MISINFORMATION POLICY

YouTube doesn't allow content about COVID-19 that poses a serious risk of egregious harm.

YouTube doesn't allow content that spreads medical misinformation that contradicts the World Health Organization (WHO) or local health authorities' medical information about COVID-19. This is limited to content that contradicts WHO or local health authorities' guidance on:

- Treatment
- Prevention
- Diagnostic
- Transmission

Note: YouTube's policies on COVID-19 are subject to change in response to changes to global or local health authorities' guidance on the virus. This policy was published on May 20, 2020.

WHAT THIS POLICY MEANS FOR YOU

If you're posting content: Don't post content on YouTube if it includes any of the following:

– Treatment Misinformation: Discourages someone from seeking medical treatment by encouraging the use of cures or remedies to treat COVID-19.
  - Claims that COVID-19 doesn't exist or that people do not die from it
  - Content that encourages the use of home remedies in place of medical treatment such as consulting a doctor or going to the hospital
  - Content that encourages the use of prayer or rituals in place of medical treatment
  - Content that claims that a vaccine for coronavirus is available or that there's a guaranteed cure
  - Content that claims that any currently-available medicine prevents you from getting the coronavirus
  - Other content that discourages people from consulting a medical professional or seeking medical advice
– Prevention Misinformation: Content that promotes prevention methods that contradict WHO or local health authorities.
– Diagnostic Misinformation: Content that promotes diagnostic methods that contradict WHO or local health authorities.

– <u>Transmission Misinformation</u>: Content that promotes transmission information that contradicts WHO or local health authorities.
  - Content that claims that COVID-19 is not caused by a viral infection
  - Content that claims COVID-19 is not contagious
  - Content that claims that COVID-19 cannot spread in certain climates or geographies
  - Content that claims that any group or individual has guaranteed immunity to the virus or cannot transmit the virus
  - Content that disputes the efficacy of WHO or local health authorities' guidance on physical distancing or self-isolation measures to reduce transmission of COVID-19

Examples: Here are some examples of content that's not allowed on YouTube:

– Denial that COVID-19 exists
– Claims that people have not died from COVID-19
– Claims that there's a guaranteed vaccine for COVID-19
– Claims that a specific treatment or medicine is a guaranteed cure for COVID-19
– Claims that certain people have immunity to COVID-19 due to their race or nationality
– Encouraging taking home remedies instead of getting medical treatment when sick
– Discouraging people from consulting a medical professional if they're sick
– Content that claims that holding your breath can be used as a diagnostic test for COVID-19
– Videos alleging that if you avoid Asian food, you won't get the coronavirus

- Videos alleging that setting off fireworks can clean the air of the virus
- Claims that COVID-19 is caused by radiation from 5G networks
- Videos alleging that the COVID-19 test is the cause of the virus
- Claims that countries with hot climates will not experience the spread of the virus
- Videos alleging that social distancing and self-isolation are not effective in reducing the spread of the virus

Notes

...

CHAPTER ONE

1. *See* Schenk v. United States, 249 U.S. 47, 52 (1919).

2. *See* W. Va. State Bd. of Educ. v. Barnette, 319 U.S. 624, 641 (1943).

3. *See* WILLIAM BLAKE, THE PORTABLE BLAKE (Alfred Kazin ed., 1977).

4. ST. AUGUSTINE, TREATISES ON VARIOUS SUBJECTS (THE FATHERS OF THE CHURCH, VOLUME 16) 78 (Roy J. Deferrari ed., 2010).

5. *See* United States v. Alvarez, 567 U.S. 709, 723 (2012) (plurality opinion) (striking down the Stolen Valor Act, which criminalized false claims about having military medals).

6. Long ago, Frederick Schauer rightly noted that "we have, perhaps surprisingly, arrived at a point in history in which an extremely important social issue about the proliferation of demonstrable factual falsity in public debate is one as to which the venerable and inspiring history of freedom of expression has virtually nothing to say." Frederick Schauer, *Facts and the First Amendment*, 57 UCLA L. REV. 897, 908 (2010). The statement remains largely true today.

7. 376 U.S. 254 (1964).

8. Hannah Arendt, *Truth and Politics*, *in* TRUTH: ENGAGEMENTS ACROSS PHILOSOPHICAL TRADITIONS 295, 297 (José Medina & David Wood eds., 2008).

CHAPTER TWO

1. *See* Whitney v. California, 274 U.S. 357, 398 (1927) (Brandeis, J., concurring).

CHAPTER THREE

1. For an accessible overview, see SISSELA BOK, LYING (1978). For an influential treatment, see WILLIAM DAVID ROSS, THE RIGHT AND THE GOOD (1930). For a valuable and provocative account, see SEANA SHIFFRIN, SPEECH MATTERS (2016).

2. *See* Arnold Isenberg, *Deontology and the Ethics of Lying*, 24 PHIL. & PHENOMENOLOGICAL RES. 463, 466 (1964). Isenberg adds: "The essential parts of the lie, according to our definition, are three. (1) A statement—and we may or may not wish to divide this again into two parts—a proposition and an utterance. (2) A disbelief or a lack of belief on the part of the speaker. (3) An intention on the part of the speaker." *Id*.

3. SHIFFRIN, *supra* note 1, at 116. For a broader definition, see THOMAS L. CARSON, LYING AND DECEPTION 15 (2010): "A lie is a deliberate false statement that the speaker warrants to be true." Carson "does not require that the liar intends to deceive others"; he recognizes that his definition does not fit with standard ones.

4. A person might, for example, misdescribe his tastes or his past in order to ingratiate himself, or in order to seem interesting.

5. For valuable discussion, see SHIFFRIN, *supra* note 1, on "pure lies."

6. See BOK, *supra* note 1, for a discussion of absolutist or near-absolutist positions with respect to lies and lying; see also Christine Korsgaard, What's Wrong with Lying (unpublished manuscript), https://www.people.fas. harvard.edu/~korsgaar/CMK.WWLying.pdf, for what is easily taken as a near-absolute ban on lying, on Kantian grounds.

7. *See* Thomas Nagel, *Concealment and Exposure*, 27 PHIL. & PUB. AFF. 3 (1998).

8. See BOK, *supra* note 1, for a discussion of white lies; Bok is more skeptical of them, on ethical grounds, than I would be, but she recognizes that some white lies are unobjectionable.

9. SHIFFRIN, *supra* note 1, offers a distinctive argument against lying. She emphasizes that it is through communication that human beings share the contents of their minds with one another. Such sharing, she urges, is essential to our identity and development as moral agents. The distinctive function of sharing is, on her view, the clue to the wrongness of lying: Liars pervert the role of communication as the mechanism by which we share what we think. Lying "transforms a mechanism for exclusively conveying the truth into a mechanism for conveying both the false and the true." *Id.* at 23. Interestingly, Augustine spoke in very similar terms: "Now it is evident that speech was given to man, not that men might therewith deceive one another, but that one man might make known his thoughts to another. To use speech, then, for the purpose of deception, and not for its appointed end, is a sin." St. Augustine, *The Enchiridian, in* THE DOCTRINAL TREATISES 251 (Jazzybe Verlang ed., 2017). One need not dispute Shiffrin's claims about the role of communication to be puzzled about her claim about what makes lying wrong. In my view, perversion of the usual mechanism for conveying truth is not an independent reason to object to lying. We need to specify a wrong that lie *does*, to actual people, in order to deem lying wrong. Compare: To use a rug as an ashtray is not a moral wrong, unless it produces a fire. (I am aware that this is just a gesture toward an engagement with Shiffrin's careful and detailed argument.)

10. I will speak throughout of utilitarianism, but we could readily use the term "welfarism," which is more capacious and which does not carry with it some of the baggage of utilitarianism. Those who prefer welfarism to utilitarianism might simply substitute that term. For discussion, see MATTHEW ADLER, WELFARE AND FAIR DISTRIBUTION (2012).

11. JEREMY BENTHAM, THE PRINCIPLES OF MORALS AND LEGISLATION 233 (1789).

12. Henry Sidgwick, *The Classification of Duties: Veracity, in* THE METHODS OF ETHICS 316 (1962 ed.)

13. Cited by his secretary, in a letter in Max Lenz, ed., *Briefwechsel Landgraf Phillips des Grossmuthigen von Hessen mit Bucer*, Vol. 1.

14. *See* EDNA ULLMANN-MARGALIT, NORMAL RATIONALITY (2017).

15. BOK, *supra* note 1, at 80.

16. *See* JOHN STUART MILL, ON LIBERTY.

17. Friedrich Hayek, *The Market and Other Orders, in* THE COLLECTED WORKS OF F. A. HAYEK 384 (Bruce Caldwell ed., 2013).

18. Behavioral economics raises important qualifications. *See* Cass R. Sunstein, *Behavioral Welfare Economics*, J. BENEFIT-COST ANALYSIS (2020).

19. See BOK, *supra* note 1, for valuable engagement with an assortment of problems, with frequent reference to utilitarian balancing (even though Bok rejects the view that utilitarianism provides an adequate framework for moral assessment of lies and lying).

20. IMMANUEL KANT, FOUNDATIONS OF THE METAPHYSICS OF MORALS 429 (1785).

21. St. Augustine, *The Enchiridion*, quoted in BOK, *supra* note 1, at 35. An interesting way to handle the problems raised by flat prohibitions on lying is to suggest that one is entitled not to tell the truth if one makes a "mental reservation," by which one says to God, or to oneself, what is true. *See* BOK, *supra* note 1, at 35.

22. Immanuel Kant, *On a Supposed Right to Lie from Altruistic Motives*, in THE DOCTRINE OF VIRTUE 92–96 (Mary J. Gregor trans., 1964).

23. Immanuel Kant, *Doctrine of Virtue*, quoted in Bok, *supra* note 1, at 32.

24. *See* Korsgaard, *supra* note 6; Paul Faulkner, *What's Wrong with Lying*, 75 PHIL. & PHENOMENOLOGICAL RES. 535 (2007).

25. Korsgaard, *supra* note 6, at 1.

26. *Id.* at 18. Korsgaard's broadest argument is worth quoting at length:

More generally, there are two conditions under which your autonomy is violated. One is when force or coercion is used to make you contribute to an end. The other is when lies are used to trick you into contributing to an end. In both cases what is wrong is that you do not get to decide whether to contribute to the end or not. The conditions under which you are able to decide for yourself are that you have power over your own actions and knowledge of what is going on. Force and coercion, on the one hand, and lies, on the other, undercut these conditions. And so force and coercion and lies are, according to this view, the most fundamental forms of wrongdoing—the roots of all evil. Morality demands that we resist the ever-present temptation to *manage* things ourselves, and instead share our decisions—and so our knowledge and our power—with all who are concerned. *Id.*

27. *See* Faulkner, *supra* note 24, at 535.

28. *See* Uri Gneezy, *Deception: The Role of Consequences*, 95 Am. Econ. Rev. 384 (2005).

29. *See* Isenberg, *supra* note 2, at 475, urging "that where the offense is small enough, the concept of moral wrongness seems to become inapplicable, just as it does in the violation of some petty rules of etiquette. I once remarked to a class in ethics, in the course of a substantially true story, that I had lived a year in the city of Rochester, in a house with a front lawn. None of this was true; but I intended that the students should believe it; and they did. I corrected the lie before the hour was over. My purpose in telling it was to illustrate a point in the ethics of lying; and I thought I could do so effectively only by first 'victimizing' the class."

30. For discussion, see Bok, *supra* note 1; Korsgaard, *supra* note 6.

31. Korsgaard, *supra* note 6, at 19. Her own understanding of this exception is exceedingly narrow.

32. Francis Hutcheson, A System of Moral Philosophy (2006 ed.).

33. An illuminating objection comes from Korsgaard, *supra* note 6, at 9, urging that the utilitarian "view does not provide a very coherent explanation of why paternalistic lies are usually wrong. For on this view, the reason not to tell paternalistic lies is that people are the best judges of what constitutes and promotes their own good. But for consequentialism to work, we must have an objective and empirically determinable notion of what is good. And once we have such a notion, it looks as if it is going to be possible for some people to be experts about the good life." Korsgaard adds: "The consequentialist view leaves too much scope for telling paternalistic lies. As I have said, it is not even clear that there is a general presumption against them. Yet most of us think that there is. When somebody lies to you for your own good, and you find out about it, you usually think the liar is a presumptuous busybody, and you resent his action. Paternalism is considered out of line when we are dealing with normal sane and healthy adults." *Id.* at 10. Insofar as Korsgaard relies on what "most of us think," I do not believe that her argument is convincing. She might be referring to a moral heuristic, one that usually works well and that must be defended on utilitarian grounds. (That is my preferred account.) Insofar as Korsgaard relies on skepticism about "an objective and empirically demonstrable notion of what is good," I think she is too skeptical. To be sure, Millian strictures

about the importance of deferring to choosers are an important reason to adopt a strong presumption against paternalistic lies—on utilitarian grounds. Korsgaard refers to those strictures, *see id.* at 11, but her response seems to me too brisk: "But the fact is that the consequentialist theory affords us no grounds for making this kind of claim. Consequentialists do not care who makes the mistakes but only how bad they are. The idea that it is better for people who make their own mistakes really comes from our third view," which is Kantian.

34. *See* Joshua Greene, *Beyond Point and Shoot Morality: Why Cognitive Neuro(Science) Matters for Ethics*, 124 ETHICS 695 (2014).

35. *See id.*; Cass R. Sunstein, *Moral Heuristics*, 28 BEHAV. & BRAIN SCIS. 531 (2005).

36. I mean this as a concern about the illuminating discussion in BOK, *supra* note 1, from which I have learned a great deal. In objecting to utilitarian approaches to lying, Bok also can be taken not to take account of the very wide range of relevant consequences, which tend to firm up, rather than to weaken, the moral taboo on lying, defended on utilitarian grounds.

37. *See* Bernard Williams, *Persons, Character, and Morality*, in MORAL LUCK 214 (1982). An instructive discussion is Elinor Mason, *Do Consequentialists Have One Thought Too Many?*, 2 ETHICAL THEORY & MORAL PRACTICE 243 (1999).

38. For an illuminating discussion and a plea for more legal intervention, see JILL HASDAY, INTIMATE LIES AND THE LAW (2019).

39. *See* NICHOLAS HATZIS, LYING, SPEECH AND IMPERSONAL HARM, LAW AND PHILOSOPHY (2019).

40. A valuable discussion is Martin H. Redish & Julio Pereyra, *Resolving the First Amendment's Civil War: Political Fraud and the Democratic Goals of Free Expression*, 62 ARIZ. L. REV. 451 (2020).

CHAPTER FOUR

1. *See generally* JOHAN FARKAS & JANNICK SCHOU, POST-TRUTH, FAKE NEWS AND DEMOCRACY (2020).

2. *See* Robert S. Mueller, III, US DEP'T OF JUSTICE, REPORT ON THE INVESTIGATION INTO RUSSIAN INTERFERENCE IN THE 2016 PRESIDENTIAL

ELECTION 14 (2019), https://www.justice.gov/storage/report.pdf [https:// perma.cc/PPD7-96ZC].

3. *Community Standards*, FACEBOOK, https://www.facebook.com/ communitystandards/integrity_authenticity (last visited July 16, 2020).

4. *False News*, FACEBOOK, https://www.facebook.com/ communitystandards/false_news (last visited July 16, 2020). One of Facebook's strategies here is to "empower[] people to decide for themselves what to read, trust, and share by informing them with more context and promoting news literacy." *Id.* There is much more to do in this vein.

5. *See* Emily Birnbaum & Olivia Beavers, *Americans Mimic Russian Disinformation Tactics Ahead of 2020*, HILL (May 8, 2019, 6:00 AM), https:// thehill.com/policy/cybersecurity/442620-americans-mimic-russian-disinformation-tactics-ahead-of-2020 [https://perma.cc/944D-ZM43].

6. *Id.*

7. *See* Robert Chesney & Danielle Citron, *Deep Fakes: A Looming Challenge for Privacy, Democracy, and National Security*, 107 CALIF. L. REV. 1753, 1757 (2019).

8. *See* Illinois *ex rel.* Madigan v. Telemarketing Assocs., Inc., 538 U.S. 600, 612 (2003) ("Like other forms of public deception, fraudulent charitable solicitation is unprotected speech"); BE&K Constr. Co. v. NLRB, 536 U.S. 516, 531 (2002) ("False statements may be unprotected for their own sake"); Hustler Magazine, Inc. v. Falwell, 485 U.S. 46, 52 (1988) ("False statements of fact are particularly valueless; they interfere with the truth-seeking function of the marketplace of ideas, and they cause damage to an individual's reputation that cannot easily be repaired by counterspeech, however persuasive or effective"); Keeton v. Hustler Magazine, Inc., 465 U.S. 770, 776 (1984) ("There is 'no constitutional value in false statements of fact'" (quoting Gertz v. Robert Welch, Inc., 418 U.S. 323, 340 (1974))); Bill Johnson's Rests., Inc. v. NLRB, 461 U.S. 731, 743 (1983) ("False statements are not immunized by the First Amendment right to freedom of speech"); Herbert v. Lando, 441 U.S. 153, 171 (1979) ("Spreading false information in and of itself carries no First Amendment credentials"); Va. State Bd. of Pharmacy v. Va. Citizens Consumer Council, Inc., 425 U.S. 748, 771 (1976) ("Untruthful speech, commercial or otherwise, has never been protected for its own sake"); *Gertz*, 418 U.S. at 340 ("The erroneous statement of fact is not worthy of constitutional protection"); Time, Inc. v. Hill, 385 U.S. 374, 389 (1967) ("The constitutional guarantees [of the First Amendment] can

tolerate sanctions against *calculated* falsehood without significant impairment of their essential function"); Garrison v. Louisiana, 379 U.S. 64, 75 (1964) ("The knowingly false statement and the false statement made with reckless disregard of the truth, do not enjoy constitutional protection").

9. 567 U.S. 709 (2012).

10. *Id.* at 723 (citing George Orwell, NINETEEN EIGHTY-FOUR (1949) (Centennial ed. (2003))).

11. *See* R.A.V. v. City of St. Paul, 505 US 377 (1992).

12. There are some complexities here. For a subtle discussion, see SEANA SHIFFRIN, SPEECH MATTERS 125–132 (2016).

13. For objections, see Derek E. Bambauer, *Shopping Badly: Cognitive Biases, Communications, and the Fallacy of the Marketplace of Ideas*, 77 U. COLO. L. REV. 649 (2006); Vincent Blasi, *Holmes and the Marketplace of Ideas*, 2004 SUP. CT. REV. 1; Paul H. Brietzke, *How and Why the Marketplace of Ideas Fails*, 31 VAL. U. L. REV. 951 (1997); R. H. Coase, *Advertising and Free Speech*, 6 J. LEGAL STUD. 1 (1977); R. H. Coase, *The Market for Goods and the Market for Ideas*, 64 AM. ECON. REV. 384 (1974); Aaron Director, *The Parity of the Economic Market Place*, 7 J.L. & ECON. 1 (1964); Stanley Ingber, *The Marketplace of Ideas: A Legitimizing Myth*, 1984 DUKE L.J. 1 (1984); William P. Marshall, *In Defense of the Search for Truth as a First Amendment Justification*, 30 GA. L. REV. 1 (1995).

14. Abrams v. United States, 250 U.S. 616, 630 (1919) (Holmes, J., dissenting).

15. *Alvarez*, 567 U.S. at 719 (plurality opinion).

16. *Id.* at 742–43 (Alito, J., dissenting).

17. As the *Alvarez* Court pointed out, there are a few "historic and traditional categories" of speech where content-based restrictions are permissible. *Id.* at 717 (quoting United States v. Stevens, 559 U.S. 460, 468 (2010)). These categories include, but are not limited to, speech "intended, and likely, to incite imminent lawless action, obscenity, defamation, speech integral to criminal conduct, [and] so-called 'fighting words.'" *Id.*

18. 567 U.S. at 720–21.

19. *Id.* at 721.

20. Frederick Schauer, *Facts and the First Amendment*, 57 UCLA L. REV. 897, 911 (2010) (explaining that despite such research, "free speech claimants . . . trot out the tired old cliches that are little more than modern

variants on Milton's now-legendary but almost certainly inaccurate paean to the pervasiveness and power of human rationality").

21. *See, e.g.*, Nina Berman, *The Victims of Fake News*, COLUM. JOURNALISM REV. (2017), https://www.cjr.org/special_report/fake-news-pizzagate-seth-rich-newtown-sandy-hook.php [https://perma.cc/J3RN-6UAH] (interviewing victims and subjects of fake news).

22. *See, e.g.*, Matthew F. Ferraro & Jason C. Chipman, *Fake News Threatens Our Businesses, Not Just Our Politics*, WASH. POST (Feb. 8, 2019, 1:33 PM), https://www.washingtonpost.com/outlook/fake-news-threatens-our-businesses-not-just-our-politics/2019/02/08/f669b62c-2b1f-11e9-984d-9b8fba003e81_story.html [https://perma.cc/AWF3-ZBTH].

23. *See, e.g.*, Claire Atkinson, *Fake News Can Cause "Irreversible Damage" to Companies—And Sink Their Stock Price*, NBC NEWS (Apr. 25, 2019, 12:54 PM), https://www.nbcnews.com/business/business-news/fake-news-can-cause-irreversible-damage-companies-sink-their-stock-n995436 [https://perma.cc/8JQ8-JDTH].

24. McKee v. Cosby, 139 S. Ct. 675, 679 (2019) (Thomas, J., concurring in the denial of certiorari).

25. Commonwealth v. Clap, 4 Mass. (3 Tyng) 163, 169–70 (1808).

26. Edward L. Glaser & Cass R. Sunstein, *Extremism and Social Learning*, 1 J. LEGAL ANALYSIS 263, 265 (2009). Of course it is also true that the source of the information matters, especially if it is drawn to people's attention. If cigarette companies say that the risks of cigarette smoking are small, people are not likely to be much moved.

27. *See* Danielle Polage, *The Effect of Telling Lies on Belief in the Truth*, 13 EUR.'s J. PSYCHOL. 633, 639 (2017).

28. *See* DANIEL KAHNEMAN, THINKING, FAST AND SLOW 20 (2011).

29. United States v. Alvarez, 567 U.S. 709, 733 (2012) (Breyer, J., concurring).

CHAPTER FIVE

1. *See generally* JOHN STUART MILL, ON LIBERTY AND THE SUBJECTION OF WOMEN 22–63 (Alan Ryan ed., Penguin Books 2006) (1859).

2. 567 U.S. 709, 733 (2012) (Breyer, J., concurring).

3. *See, e.g.*, Heiko Rauhut, *Beliefs about Lying and Spreading of Dishonesty: Undetected Lies and Their Constructive and Destructive Social Dynamics in Dice Experiments*, 8 PLOS ONE 1, 5 (2013).

4. *See* EDNA ULLMANN-MARGALIT, THE EMERGENCE OF NORMS 14 (1977).

5. *See* Jud Campbell, *Natural Rights and the First Amendment*, 127 YALE L.J. 246 (2017).

6. *See* ALEXANDER MEIKLEJOHN, FREE SPEECH AND ITS RELATION TO SELF-GOVERNMENT (1948).

7. Thomas Scanlon, *A Theory of Freedom of Expression*, 1 PHIL. & PUB. AFF. 204 (1972).

8. *See* SEANA SHIFFRIN, SPEECH MATTERS (2016).

9. *Id.* at 117.

10. MILL, *supra* note 1, at 24.

11. *The Criminalization of COVID-19 Clicks and Conspiracies*, MEDIUM (May 13, 2020), https://medium.com/dfrlab/op-ed-the-criminalization-of-covid-19-clicks-and-conspiracies-3af077f5a7e7.

12. 18 U.S.C. § 1621 (2012).

13. 15 U.S.C. § 54 (2012).

14. 18 U.S.C. § 1001.

15. 18 U.S.C. § 912 ("Whoever falsely assumes or pretends to be an officer or employee acting under the authority of the United States or any department, agency or officer thereof, and acts as such . . . shall be fined under this title or imprisoned").

16. 567 U.S. 709, 723 (2012).

17. *Id.* at 731–32 (Breyer, J., concurring).

18. *Id.* at 751–52 (Alito, J., dissenting).

19. JOSEPH RAZ, ETHICS IN THE PUBLIC DOMAIN 39 (1994).

20. *See* Dun & Bradstreet, Inc. v. Greenmoss Builders, Inc., 472 U.S. 749, 763 (1985).

21. MILL, *supra* note 1, at 42–44.

22. *Id.* at 23.

23. SHIFFRIN, *supra* note 8, at 140–144.

24. *See* United States v. Chappell, 691 F.3d 388 (4th Cir. 2012) (ruling that the First Amendment does not ban the "Virginia police impersonation statute, . . . [which] prohibits individuals from falsely assuming or pretending to be a law enforcement officer").

25. SHIFFRIN, *supra* note 8, at 141.

26. *See* Xavier Gabaix, *Behavioral Inattention* 5 (Nat'l. Bureau of Econ. Research, Working Paper No. 24096, 2018).

27. *See* Cass R. Sunstein, Sebastian Bobadilla-Suarez, Stephanie C. Lazzaro, & Tali Sharot, *How People Update Beliefs about Climate Change: Good News and Bad News*, 102 CORNELL L. REV. 1431, 1433 (2017).

28. *See* TIMUR KURAN, PUBLIC LIES, PRIVATE TRUTHS 78 (1997).

29. *See* Dennis v. United States, 341 U.S. 494, 503 (1951).

30. 395 U.S. 444 (1969).

CHAPTER SIX

1. Myrto Pantazi, Olivier Klein, & Mikhail Kissine, *Is Justice Blind or Myopic?* 15 JUDGEMENT & DECISION MAKING 214 (2020), available at http://journal.sjdm.org/19/190118a/jdm190118a.pdf.

2. *Id.*

3. *Id.*

4. Soroush Vosoughi, Deb Roy, & Sinan Aral, *The Spread of True and False News Online*, 359 SOC. SCI., available at https://science.sciencemag.org/content/359/6380/1146

5. Chip Heath, Chris Bell, & Emily Sternberg, *Emotional Selection in Memes: The Case of Urban Legends*, 81 J. PERSONALITY & SOC. PSYCHOL. 1028 (2001), available at http://citeseerx.ist.psu.edu/viewdoc/download?doi=10.1.1.627.1473&rep=rep1&type=pdf.

6. *See* Brendan Nyhan & Jason Reifler, *When Corrections Fail: The Persistence of Political Misconceptions*, 32 POL. BEHAV. 303, 308–309 (2010).

7. *See* Thomas Wood & Ethan Porter, *The Elusive Backfire Effect*, 41 POL. BEHAV. 135 (2019).

8. *See* the overview in Solomon Asch, *Opinions and Social Pressure*, in READINGS ABOUT THE SOCIAL ANIMAL 13 (Elliott Aronson ed., 1995).

9. I draw in the following sections on CASS R. SUNSTEIN, CONFORMITY (2019), adapting the discussion there for present purposes.

10. *Id.* at 15.

11. Dominic Abrams et al., *Knowing What to Think by Knowing Who You Are*, 29 BRIT. J. SOC. PSYCHOL. 97, 106–108 (1990).

12. *Id.*

13. *See* ROBERT SHILLER, IRRATIONAL EXUBERANCE 149–50 (2000).

14. *See* Rod Bond & Peter Smith, *Culture and Conformity: A Meta-Analysis of Studies Using Asch's Line Judgement Task,* 199 PSYCHOL. BULL. 111, 124 (1996).

15. *See* ROBERT BARON ET AL., GROUP PROCESS, GROUP DECISION, GROUP ACTION 66 (2d ed. 1999).

16. Asch, supra 116, at 21.

17. *Id.*

18. *See, e.g.,* Sushil Biikhchandani et al., *Learning from the Behavior of Others,* J. ECON. PERSP., Summer 1998, at 151; Lisa Anderson & Charles Holt, *Information Cascades in the Laboratory,* 87 AM. ECON. REV. 847 (1997); Abhijit Banerjee, *A Simple Model of Herd Behavior,* 107 Q.J. ECON. 797 (1992); Andrew Daughety & Jennifer Reinganum, *Stampede to Judgment,* 1 AM. L. & ECON. REV. 158, 159–65 (1999).

19. *See* Mark Granovetter, *Threshold Models of Collective Behavior,* 83 AM. J. SOC. 1420 (1978); for a recent popular treatment, see MALCOLM GLADWELL, THE TIPPING POINT 5–22 (2000).

20. *See* Lisa Anderson & Charles Holt, *Information Cascades in the Laboratory,* 87 AM. ECON. REV. 847 (1997).

21. *See* TIMUR KURAN, PUBLIC LIES, PRIVATE TRUTHS 4–20 (1997).

22. THE FEDERALIST No. 49 (James Madison).

23. *See* Cass R. Sunstein, *The Law of Group Polarization,* 10 J. POLIT. PHIL. 175 (2002).

24. *See* ROGER BROWN, SOCIAL PSYCHOLOGY 222 (2d ed. 1985). These include the United States, Canada, New Zealand, Germany, and France. *See, e.g.,* Johannes Zuber et al., *Choice Shift and Group Polarization,* 62 J. PERSONALITY & SOC. PSYCHOL. 50 (1992) (Germany); Abrams, *supra* note 11, at 112 (New Zealand). Of course it is possible that some cultures would show a greater or lesser tendency toward polarization; this would be an extremely interesting area for empirical study.

25. *See* D. G. Myers, *Discussion-Induced Attitude Polarization,* 28 HUM. REL. 699 (1975).

26. BROWN, *supra* note 24, at 224.

27. D. G. Myers and G. D. Bishop, *The Enhancement of Dominant Attitudes in Group Discussion,* 20 J. PERSONALITY & SOC. PSYCHOL. 286 (1976).

28. *See id.*

CHAPTER SEVEN

1. *See, e.g.,* JULIANNE SCHULTZ, REVIVING THE FOURTH ESTATE: DEMOCRACY, ACCOUNTABILITY AND THE MEDIA 47–68 (1998).

2. Cass R. Sunstein, Sebastian Bobadilla-Suarez, Stephanie C. Lazzaro, & Tali Sharot, *How People Update Beliefs about Climate Change: Good News and Bad News*, 102 CORNELL L. REV. 1431, 1440 (2017); *see also* Michael Thaler, *The "Fake News" Effect: An Experiment on Motivated Reasoning and Trust in News* 33 (Nov. 1, 2019) (unpublished manuscript) (on file with author). An important finding, specifying motivated reasoning, involves "desirability bias" in belief updating. Ben Tappin et al., *The Heart Trumps the Head: Desirability Bias in Political Belief Revision*, 146 J. EXP. PSYCHOL. 1143, 1147 (2017).

3. Jud Campbell, *Natural Rights and the First Amendment*, 127 YALE L.J. 246 (2017).

4. 376 U.S. 254 (1964). On the history of libel, *see generally* William L. Prosser, *Libel Per Quod*, 46 VA. L. REV. 839 (1960).

5. McKee v. Cosby, 139 S. Ct. 675, 678 (2019) (Thomas, J., concurring in the denial of certiorari). The literature on the case is voluminous. *See generally* KERMIT HALL & MELVIN UROFSKY, *NEW YORK TIMES V. SULLIVAN*: CIVIL RIGHTS, LIBEL LAW, AND THE FREE PRESS (2011); ANTHONY LEWIS, MAKE NO LAW: THE SULLIVAN CASE AND THE FIRST AMENDMENT (1991); Richard A. Epstein, *Was* New York Times v. Sullivan *Wrong?*, 53 U. CHI. L. REV. 782 (1986). For a valuable historical perspective, see James Maxwell Koffler, *The Pre-Sullivan Common Law Web of Protection against Political Defamation Suits*, 47 HOFSTRA L. REV. 153 (2018).

6. *See* HARRY KALVEN, THE NEGRO AND THE FIRST AMENDMENT 55 (1965).

7. 376 U.S. at 280, 286–87; *see also* Dun & Bradstreet, Inc. v. Greenmoss Builders, Inc., 472 U.S. 749, 776 (1985) (Brennan, J., dissenting).

8. 376 U.S. at 271–72 (quoting NAACP v. Button, 371 U.S. 415, 433 (1963)).

9. *Id.* at 273.

10. *See* Epstein, *supra* note 5, at 806.

11. 418 U.S. 323 (1974).

12. *Id.* at 341.

13. 376 U.S. at 278.

14. *Id.* at 279.

15. United States v. Alvarez, 567 U.S. 709, 718 (2012).

16. *See* McKee v. Cosby, 139 S. Ct. 675, 676 (2019) (Thomas, J., concurring in the denial of certiorari).

17. *Id.*

18. Pub. L. No. 105-304, 112 Stat. 2860 (1998) (codified in scattered sections of 17 U.S.C.).

19. 47 U.S.C. § 230 (2012).

20. For an interesting perspective, see Adi Robertson, *Why the Internet's Most Important Law Exists and How People Are Still Getting It Wrong,* THE VERGE (June 21, 2019, 1:02 PM), https://www.theverge.com/2019/6/21/18700605/section-230-internet-law-twenty-six-words-that-created-the-internet-jeff-kosseff-interview [https://perma.cc/WT9S-6Q3C].

21. *See, e.g.,* Batzel v. Smith, 333 F.3d 1018, 1034 (9th Cir. 2003); Zeran v. Am. Online Inc., 129 F.3d 327, 331 (4th Cir. 1997); Blumenthal v. Drudge, 992 F. Supp. 44, 49–53 (D.D.C. 1998); Barrett v. Rosenthal, 146 P.3d 510, 513 (Cal. 2006).

22. *See* Patricia Sanchez Abril & Jacqueline D. Lipton, *The Right to Be Forgotten: Who Decides What the World Forgets?,* 103 KY. L.J. 363, 385 (2014).

23. *See Bullying and Harassment,* FACEBOOK COMMUNITY STANDARDS, https://www.facebook.com/communitystandards/bullying [https://perma.cc/DD63-GZQY].

CHAPTER EIGHT

1. *See* Hannah Arendt, *Truth and Politics, in* TRUTH: ENGAGEMENTS ACROSS PHILOSOPHICAL TRADITIONS 295, 300 (José Medina & David Wood eds., 2008).

2. *See generally* Gerald G. Ashdown, *Distorting Democracy: Campaign Lies in the 21st Century,* 20 WM. & MARY BILL RTS. J. 1085 (2012); William P. Marshall, *False Campaign Speech and the First Amendment,* 153 U. PA. L. REV. 285 (2004).

3. I am bracketing here the possibility that some imaginable statutes regulating falsehoods could turn out to be a form of content discrimination or viewpoint discrimination. For example, a ban on falsehoods about

Republican candidates, but not Democratic candidates, could easily be seen as impermissible content discrimination. A ban on falsehoods about the president of the United States might well fall in the same category. There are some tricky issues here. A ban on threats against the president is generally taken to be constitutional, evidently on the ground that such threats have a content-neutral justification; threats against the commander in chief are uniquely harmful. Can the same thing be said about falsehoods? In my view, that conclusion would be hard to justify. A ban on falsehoods involving a particular official, even the president, would be best understood as an effort to protect him from scrutiny.

4. *See* Pestrak v. Ohio Elections Comm'n., 926 F.2d 573, 577 (6th Cir. 1991) (upholding an Ohio statute banning false statements in political campaigns). *But see* Susan B. Anthony List v. Driehaus, 814 F.3d 466, 476 (6th Cir. 2016) (striking down an Ohio election-lies law as a content-based restriction of "core political speech" that lacked sufficient tailoring); 281 Care Comm. v. Arneson, 766 F.3d 774, 785 (8th Cir. 2014) ("[N]o amount of narrow tailoring succeeds because [Minnesota's political false-statements law] is not necessary, is simultaneously overbroad and underinclusive, and is not the least restrictive means of achieving any stated goal."); Tomei v. Finley, 512 F. Supp. 695, 698 (N.D. Ill. 1981) (holding that the use of "REP" in the election context was not protected by the First Amendment because it falsely suggested that the defendants were Republicans). For arguments that such restrictions should be invalidated, see Marshall, *supra* note 2, at 300–22; Geoffrey R. Stone, *The Rules of Evidence and the Rules of Public Debate*, U. CHI. LEGAL F. 127, 136–37 (1993); James Weinstein, *Free Speech and Domain Allocation: A Suggested Framework for Analyzing the Constitutionality of Prohibitions of Lies*, 71 OKLA. L. REV. 167, 206–13 (2018).

5. Leonardo Bursztyn, Aakaash Rao, Christopher Roth, & David Yanagizawa-Drott, *Misinformation during a Pandemic* (Becker Friedman Institute, Working Paper No. 2020-44, 2020), https://bfi.uchicago.edu/wp-content/uploads/BFI_WP_202044.pdf.

6. Marc Jonathan Blitz, *Lies, Line Drawing, and (Deep) Fake News*, 71 OKLA. L. REV. 59, 61 (2018); Robert Chesney & Danielle Citron, *Deep Fakes: A Looming Challenge for Privacy, Democracy, and National Security*, 107 CALIF. L. REV. 1753, 1757–58 (2019).

7. Danielle Keats Citron, *Sexual Privacy*, 128 YALE L.J. 1870, 1921–22 (2019).

8. *See, e.g.*, BBC News, *Fake Obama Created Using AI Video Tool*, YOUTUBE (July 19, 2017), https://www.youtube.com/watch?v=AmUC4m6w1wo [https://perma.cc/89DT-Y4C6]; Fortune Magazine, *What Is a Deepfake? Video Examples with Nicolas Cage, Jennifer Lawrence, Obama Show Troubling Trend*, YOUTUBE (Mar. 11, 2019), https://www.youtube.com/watch?v=-yQxsIWO2ic [https://perma.cc/WW9F-JZ9F]; Bernhard Warner, *Deepfake Video of Mark Zuckerberg Goes Viral on Eve of House A.I. Hearing*, FORTUNE (June 12, 2019, 12:31 PM), https://fortune.com/2019/06/12/deepfake-mark-zuckerberg [https://perma.cc/52PM-2DGE].

9. Corp. Training Unlimited, Inc. v. Nat'l. Broad. Co., 868 F. Supp. 501, 507 (E.D.N.Y. 1994) (explaining that when scrutinizing "audio and video portions of a television program," courts should be cognizant of "the possibility that a transcript which appears relatively mild on its face may actually be . . . highly toxic," and that "a clever amalgamation of half-truths and opinion-like statements, adorned with orchestrated images and dramatic audio accompaniment, can be devastating when packaged in the powerful television medium").

10. In *Alvarez*, Justice Breyer noted that "few statutes, if any, simply prohibit without limitation the telling of a lie, even a lie about one particular matter. Instead, in virtually all these instances limitations of context, requirements of proof of injury, and the like, narrow the statute to a subset of lies where specific harm is more likely to occur." 567 U.S. 709, 736 (2012) (Breyer, J., concurring). He continued by explaining that "the limitations help to make certain that the statute does not allow its threat of liability or criminal punishment to roam at large, discouraging or forbidding the telling of the lie in contexts where harm is unlikely or the need for the prohibition is small." *Id.*

11. Hustler Magazine, Inc. v. Falwell, 485 U.S. 46, 54 (1988).

12. Even if deepfakes did not threaten to harm their subjects, they could nonetheless cause harm. Consider, for example, a deepfake that portrays a political candidate as doing something heroic when he did nothing of the kind.

13. *Alvarez*, 567 U.S. at 727.

14. Yoel Roth & Ashita Achuthan, *Building Rules in Public: Our Approach to Synthetic & Manipulated Media*, TWITTER BLOG (Feb. 4, 2020), https://blog.twitter.com/en_us/topics/company/2020/new-approach-to-synthetic-and-manipulated-media.html. The blog post elaborates:

Some specific harms we consider include:—Threats to the physical safety of a person or group—Risk of mass violence or widespread civil unrest—Threats to the privacy or ability of a person or group to freely express themselves or participate in civic events, such as: stalking or unwanted and obsessive attention; targeted content that includes tropes, epithets, or material that aims to silence someone; voter suppression or intimidation.

15. *Alvarez*, 567 U.S. at 726.

16. *Id.* at 729.

17. For a valuable discussion, see generally Blitz, *supra* note 6 ("[W]here false statements do not merely state false facts, but are also given in a form that carries with it indicia for reliability (such as a falsified newspaper or video or audio tape), the government should have greater power to regulate than it typically has to regulate false words." *Id.* at 110.). For a careful analysis of the constitutional issues, see Chesney & Citron, *supra* note 6, at 1790–93 (finding *Alvarez* a significant obstacle to regulation).

18. *See* Daniel Kahneman, Thinking, Fast and Slow 20–21 (2011).

19. Monika Bickert, *Enforcing against Manipulated Media*, Facebook (Jan. 6, 2020), https://about.fb.com/news/2020/01/enforcing-against-manipulated-media [https://perma.cc/A4SV-878X].

20. *Id.*; *see also* Guy Rosen, *Helping to Protect the 2020 US Elections*, Facebook (Oct. 21, 2019), https://about.fb.com/news/2019/10/update-on-election-integrity-efforts [https://perma.cc/Q6DV-YA4Q] (announcing additional safeguards to reduce the impact of viral misinformation on U.S. elections).

21. *Spam, Deceptive Practices & Scams Policies*, YouTube Help Center, https://support.google.com/youtube/answer/2801973?hl=en (last visited July 16, 2020).

22. Guy Rosen et al., *Helping to Protect the 2020 US Elections*, Facebook (Oct. 21, 2019), https://about.fb.com/news/2019/10/update-on-election-integrity-efforts/.

23. *Id.*

24. *Misinformation*, Facebook, https://www.facebook.com/policies/ads/prohibited_content/misinformation.

25. *See Civic Integrity Policy*, Twitter (May 2020), https://help.twitter.com/en/rules-and-policies/election-integrity-policy.

26. *See Spam, Deceptive Practices, and Scams Policies*, *supra* note 21.

27. Yoel Roth & Nick Pickles, *Updating Our Approach to Misleading Information*, TWITTER BLOG (May 11, 2020), https://blog.twitter.com/en_us/topics/product/2020/updating-our-approach-to-misleading-information.html.

28. 376 U.S. 254 (1964).

29. 395 U.S. 444 (1969).

30. *See* Tessa Lyons, *Hard Questions: What's Facebook's Strategy for Stopping False News?* (May 23, 2018), https://about.fb.com/news/2018/05/hard-questions-false-news/.

31. *See* Alex Kantrowitz, *Facebook Is Taking Down Posts That Cause Imminent Harm—But Not Posts That Cause Inevitable Harm*, BUZZ FEED NEWS (May 23, 2020, 11:50 AM), https://www.buzzfeednews.com/article/alexkantrowitz/facebook-coronavirus-misinformation-takedowns.

32. *See* Cass R. Sunstein, *Does the Clear and Present Danger Test Survive Cost-Benefit Analysis?*, 104 CORNELL L. REV. 1775 (2019).

CHAPTER NINE

1. *See* Hannah Arendt, *Truth and Politics*, *in* TRUTH: ENGAGEMENTS ACROSS PHILOSOPHICAL TRADITIONS 295, 300 (José Medina & David Wood eds., 2008).

Index

. . .

For the benefit of digital users, indexed terms that span two pages (e.g., 52–53) may, on occasion, appear on only one of those pages.

Page numbers followed by *t* indicate tables. Numbers followed by n indicate endnotes.

INDEX